HMP MANCHESTER PRISON OFFICER

I SURVIVED
**TERRORISTS,
MURDERERS,
RAPISTS** AND
**FREEMASON
OFFICER ATTACKS**
IN STRANGEWAYS
AND WORMOOD
SCRUBS

JOHN G SUTTON

First published in Great Britain by Gadfly Press in 2022

This book is a work of non-fiction based on research by the author

A catalogue record of this book is available from the British Library

Typeset and cover design by Jane Dixon-Smith

This book is dedicated to my dear wife Mary, who had to live through these turbulent times, supporting me all the way. Thank you for believing in the impossible when the going was way beyond tough. Mary Sutton, an amazing lady, my wife.

CONTENTS

CHAPTER 1

THE INVISIBLE BROTHERHOOD

The stench of stale urine hung in the air like an invisible smog as, one by one, the inmates shuffled along the prison landing, carrying their overflowing pots, brimming with human waste.

'Get a move on!' the huge overweight jailer shouted, swinging his key chain and glowering at the degraded occupants of C2 landing, deep inside the dungeon that was London's biggest prison, HMP Wormwood Scrubs. This was my first week and, already, any ideas I had about helping prisoners to reform were fast fading away. The staff here just banged them up, slopped them out and generally treated the occupants of this dark Victorian jail like they were the enemy.

'Stop him!'

I turned and saw a huge black man running towards me. Instinctively I stepped to my right, blocking the landing between the walls of the cell and the cast iron railing. The distance between us rapidly decreased and, as the prisoner flung out his right arm to push me aside, I hit him with a solid left fist, sinking it into his solar plexus. He staggered backwards, falling to the floor clutching his stomach and gasping for breath. The fat jailer who had shouted was there now, gripping the man by his hair.

'Get him downstairs' he yelled and, between us, we dragged the prisoner along the landing, down the metal stairs and onto the first floor. There, we were met by three other jailers, who snatched hold of the man, lifted him bodily off the floor and carried him at speed to an empty cell. I ran along to help if needed but this team were experts. By the time I got there, the prisoner was on the cold stone floor, having his clothing ripped off him. By now, he was trying to scream; this had no effect, other than to earn him a blow to the face from one of the staff struggling with him. Within less than a minute, he was stripped naked, bleeding from his nose and mouth, writhing in the corner of that bare brick cell in shock.

'Welcome to The Scrubs,' the heavily-built Principal Officer said to me with a sinister laugh, as he slammed the cell door shut.

C Wing at The Scrubs was packed from bottom to top with all manner of male prisoners, from petty thieves serving three months for shop-lifting to Cat 'A' killers with multiple life sentences. I had been allocated to work on C2 landing, which housed over 200 inmates in 88 cells. It was the single largest prison landing in Europe. The officer in charge was a former Special Air Services NCO, who didn't just scare the prisoners, he scared me too. He was around six foot in height, broad shoulders, must have been 220lbs, thick curly black hair, with an obviously broken nose and a beard. His hands were heavy with muscular-looking fingers and he wore Army boots. His voice was not only loud, it echoed all around C Wing when he shouted, and he shouted a lot.

Having dealt with the crazy guy running riot, I went back up the metal stairs and continued my duties. By now, it was time for breakfast, just 7:20am and I had already been involved in violence. C2 inmates went down to the hotplate on what they called the 'Ones', collected their food on metal trays and took these back to their cells to eat.

'Bang 'em up!' yelled an officer and, soon, we had all the prisoners inside their doors and counted. 'Two hundred and three on the Twos,' he shouted down to the Senior Officer on the Ones. It was time for us to take our own breakfast break.

Inside the jail, there was an officers' canteen but it was staffed by prisoners working as cooks, preparing the food for the Prison Officers. I was not of a mind to run the risk of eating there as I suspected there would likely be some adulteration of the meals by vengeful inmates. Instead, I had an apple and some chocolate with a drink of coffee in the C Wing Kardomah, which was a single cell, used by staff to make themselves a warm drink, where there were a few seats. I got talking to two other officers; well, I tried to, but they seemed rather reluctant to speak to me. I tried asking how long each of them had been there. No reply, just a little advice, 'Mind your own business'.

That was a little dispiriting but I gave it another go; 'I just joined from Leyhill Training School, signed up at Strangeways'. Silence, nothing, just a suspicious stare from the older officer. At the time, I did not know it was standard practice at The Scrubs for the more senior staff to give new recruits the silent treatment. It certainly made me feel a little uneasy as, in the event of trouble, such as the crazy inmate this morning, I needed to count on these officers to help me. As I finished my coffee and stood up to leave the converted cell, the older officer finally spoke to me: 'I saw you dealing with that con on the Twos,' he said. 'Next time, knock the bastard out'. Charming, I thought, but maybe he had a point as, even after I had put him down, that prisoner had managed to put up quite a struggle.

My main detail for the morning was to supervise the cleaners on C1 landing, who had to empty and scrub out certain cells I had been advised required attention. These cells were occupied by seriously unsavoury prisoners, known within the jail as 'paraffin lamps', which is Cockney London rhyming slang for tramps. I collected the cleaners, trusted inmates, and they picked up their buckets, mops, brushes, carbolic soap and disinfectant. Then I opened the first cell; the stench was like walking into a recently used, unflushed lavatory. It wafted out and virtually crawled along the landing. I looked inside and saw movement in the stygian darkness; something was alive in there.

The two cleaners had obviously experienced this many times before and walked in, seemingly oblivious to the gut-wrenching smell. One at a time, the two tramps staggered out of that pit of shit and stumbled forward towards me, arms outstretched. I recoiled in horror. They were like two zombies, their ragged clothing caked in human excrement and dripping with what looked like piss. Each cleaner took one of these disgusting wretches and led them to the shower unit directly across the landing from their lair.

'Fire hose, Gov,' said one of the cleaners, pointing to a rolled-up hosepipe on the wall. At first, I did not quite understand what he meant.

'We hose them down, Gov,' he said, laughing at my incredulity.

The power from the fire hose blew the two pitiful creatures across the tiled shower unit floor, where they lay as one cleaner stripped off what passed as their clothing and the other aimed the jet of water at them. When they were both naked and the filth had been washed off them, the cleaners threw each of them a towel, turned off the hosepipe and left them to get dry, as they went to dig out the disgusting bear pit that was their cell. It seemed this routine was undertaken two or three times a week, as the tramps were doubly incontinent and unable to use toilet facilities, even if their cell had them.

Prior to being lifted off the streets of London by the police, they had been living rough, drinking whatever they could get hold of, meths mixed with coke, cheap but powerful cider, anything to get their minds out of that living hell into which they had descended. Society had abandoned all responsibility; there were no hostels that would accept vagrants such as these, no hospitals, no institutions other than the last resort, prison, and that was where they now were, languishing in their own excrement.

Following the tramp detail, I returned to C2 landing, unlocking and locking the inmates, who repeated the trip to the hotplate to collect their lukewarm cooked lunch and then returned to their cells. I was scheduled to be on late break so, while all the staff went for their mid-day meal, I patrolled the landing alone. My instructions were simple enough; do not open any cells unless there are at least two of you. I had asked what to do if a prisoner sounded an alarm and demanded to be unlocked to use the toilet.

'Look, lad, you just tell them this: 'Get on your pot'.'

The inmates were mainly three to a cell, with no facilities to relieve themselves, other than a plastic pot and a bucket. Telling anyone to just defecate in their cell in front of two other people, who would be subjected to the smell, seemed to me an abuse. I would quickly become hardened to that manner of interacting with prisoners; it was that way or the highway, as a man once said.

It was perhaps twenty minutes to 1pm when I saw the wing Governor a Mr. C. ascending the metal stairs to my landing on C2. I was some fifteen or so yards away from him when I saw he was opening a cell. Now I knew that there were certain strict rules concerning the movement of all inmates during lockdown at lunchtime and no cells should be unlocked unless in emergency.

'With due respect, sir, the wing is in lockdown for lunch and this inmate may not be moved,' I advised the Wing Governor.

'You know who I am, do you, officer?' he said, glaring at me as if I were an unpleasant object. 'Get about your duties' he growled and walked off C2 landing down on to the ones where I saw him walk with the inmate to his office at the far end of the wing.

I called down to the Senior Officer on the ones and told him what had happened, he seemed unconcerned. 'He's the Governor,' was all I got in response. But I knew that this was suspicious, so I checked the inmates cell card it showed he was doing 9 years. I did not personally know this inmate but he was obviously a serious villain to be sentenced to a long term of imprisonment. Why, I wondered, would the Wing Governor take him to his office at lunch time, in clear breach of Prison Rules. That was perhaps the start of my problems at The Scrubs, I was thinking and asking questions whilst the rest of the officers just accepted things the way they were. But I knew something was wrong here and I would, I felt sure, eventually discover exactly what.

Shortly after 1pm I saw the Wing Governor with the inmate next to him walking along the ones.

'Officer, lock him up,' he shouted to me and the prisoner walked up the stairs to his cell.

Opening the door, I asked him a direct question: 'What on earth are you doing with the Governor?'

He was a typical East End villain: big build, over 200lbs, cheeky smirk on his face and a casually offensive tone.

'I wouldn't ask if I were you, boss, way above your pay-grade'.

After locking him inside his door, I walked away wondering what on earth that was all about. But I would find out. I was determined to do that as all my instincts told me that matters here needed to be looked at. I sensed the Governor was up to no good, it just looked wrong. As I said, this incident was the start of my troubles, though at the time I did not know it I had crossed the path of a senior member of the Freemasons. Ahead of me awaited a difficult lesson as I proceeded to ask questions and seek to do what I seriously considered to be my duty. Without realising this I had observed a member of the invisible brotherhood at work; shedding light on that darkness was forbidden as I would soon discover.

Following my lunch break, I was sent from C Wing to report to the Principal Officer in charge of D Wing, as they were short-staffed for the afternoon shift. D Wing at The Scrubs was where all the life sentence and long-term inmates were located. I had been on the wing before but never worked there; it was nothing like C Wing, which was all hustle and bustle. D Wing was, on the surface at least, low-key, easy going and less stressful, at least for the inmates. The PO in charge of the wing sent me out onto the landings to patrol with this caution: 'If in any doubt, do nothing, come and see me'.

So there I was, in uniform, wandering round the lifers' wing, with orders to ignore anything that might seem to me to be questionable. What was the point, I wondered.

My first encounter was with a rather overly confident con-victed killer called Grantham. He was about my age and, having given me a once-over, asked about my Army-issue boots. When I told him I had been in the military in Germany, he immediately began giving me his tale of woe about how he accidentally shot and killed a taxi driver when he was a soldier in a German town. Grantham was amusing enough and introduced me to his friends on D Wing as, despite the fact I was now a jailer and he was a prisoner, we had something in common.

Grantham took me to meet an inmate called Gordon Goody, who had been one of the main men behind The Great Train Robbery. He was quite a gentleman and told me his sentence was coming to an end and he was intending to move away from the UK to Spain. Grantham wanted to be an actor, or so he said, as he explained how, on D Wing, there was a drama group and he had been acting in a play called 'Entertaining Mr Sloane' by Joe Orton. (Grantham went on to play the character Dirty Den in the UK TV series, Eastenders). Innocently, I asked Grantham, full name Leslie Grantham, if he had met Ian Brady, the moors murderer, who I knew to be in The Scrubs.

'You a cop?' Grantham asked me, suddenly on guard. to which I assured him I most certainly was not but asked him why he thought I might be. 'That shithouse child-killer Brady was on this wing last week, lasted two days, then someone dragged him into the recess on D3, gave him a proper beating and poured boiling water over his head.'

'No names, no pack drill,' I replied, and both Goody and Grantham found that amusing.

It was approximately 4:30pm and I had walked all over D Wing, generally observing the inmates going about their routine without incident, when the Principal Officer shouted for me. I was on the Twos at the time and quickly got myself down to the main office on the Ones.

'Go get inmate 'X' from D3-18 and bring him to me here,' the PO ordered.

Thinking nothing much about this, I walked up the steel stairs to D3 landing, found cell 18 and, in there, was an inmate I assumed to be 'X'. When I told him the PO needed to see him, he just turned and glared at me, then in a broad Irish accent, growled, 'Ya tell dat feckin' 'eedjit I'm busy.'

Well, that was not the answer I was expecting, nor was willing to accept. Forgetting I was operating on the relaxed regime of D

Wing, I reached inside the cell, grabbed 'X' by the front of his jacket and lifted him onto the landing, where I spun him round and began marching him, arm up his back, down the stairs to D1 and the PO in his office. He put up quite a degree of resistance but I had the better of it and was far too strong for him. As we approached the office, I heard a loud yell and the sound of running feet. In an instant, I was surrounded by regular D Wing officers, who blocked my route to the PO and the office.

'Let him go!' they shouted.

I was bemused.

'You let go or else!' shouted an oversized jailer with a red face and hands that were reaching for me.

Fearing for my safety, I released my grip on inmate 'X', who instantly began to abuse me in his Irish dialect, saying something like 'We knows where youse live, ya British bastard.'

As all this was happening, the Principal Officer came out of the office and up to me.

'Get off my wing,' he yelled, pointing to the iron gate leading into and out of D Wing.

The jailers standing round me moved closer and I decided that discretion was the better part of valour, so I made for the exit. Quite what that was all about, I had no idea at the time. To me, it seemed straightforward; I had given the inmate a direct order and he had refused to accept and so I had taken what I considered to be appropriate action and gripped the man. That, as I saw it, was doing my duty, simply following orders, i.e. 'Go get prisoner 'X''. So I had gone and brought that inmate as ordered and yet they were unhappy with this, for some reason that escaped me.

I made my way back to C Wing and reported to the PO that I had been ordered off D Wing. He gave me what I would call a rather old-fashioned stare.

'Mr Sutton, you have been here less than a week and I already have two complaints about your behaviour. One from the Wing Governor, who states that you were questioning his authority and now another from the PO in charge of D Wing, advising that you assaulted a prisoner. Not just any prisoner, Mr Sutton, you laid hands on the local head of the IRA. Are you trying to get yourself killed?'

I was puzzled by this. First of all, the Wing Governor was in the wrong and, as for that inmate on D Wing, as far as I was concerned, he was a prisoner and, when I give any prisoner an order, they either comply or face the consequences. It appeared I may have been mistaken as, at The Scrubs, there are unwritten rules set down by an invisible brotherhood, who were actually in command of the jail.

'Now, get out of my office,' the Principal Officer ordered, in a manner that indicated he was distinctly disturbed.

For the second time that day, I was left contemplating my position; was I really deluded, going about my duties, doing the job properly as I saw it and yet finding myself on the wrong side of matters?

That night as I lay on my bed in the lodgings where I rented a single room, I thought about what was happening to me at The Scrubs. The hours were long, 7am to 5:30pm or even 9pm on the late shift, working every other weekend. The promised housing accommodation for myself and my wife Mary had not materialised.. What kind of a dirty disgraceful job was this? How had I ended up here and why I wondered was it all going so badly? I was hardly a complete idiot. I had been an NCO in the Army, passed all the exams that were required and this was supposed to be my new career.

As I lay there pondering these problems, I thought back to the start of all this. To the time when I was still in the Army at Lark Hill considering my future. My wife Mary and I had ambition then, we had dreams. I aspired to be a writer and a poet. Mary wanted to help me do all that, but I needed a job, this was supposed to be it. On the very edge of sleep, I remembered a distant day standing by the stones at Stonehenge with Mary at my side. The rain was blowing in on the cold west wind and I looked up at the ancient mighty monolithic monument, touching its wet granite surface with my hands. I was seeking spiritual guidance with hope in my heart, asking to be shown a way to succeed. Gradually that memory faded to black and slowly, slowly, I drifted into a deeply disturbing nightmare.

CHAPTER 2

MY FATHER'S GHOST

Wiltshire, England, 1972

Early one dismal December morning, with the rain sweeping in on a cold western wind, I stood facing the stark bleakness of Stonehenge. The huge dark stones towered above me, glistening wet under a sombre slate grey sky. My wife, Mary, and I were there together, trying to tune our spiritual energies to the Neolithic magnificence of this ancient monument. We lived in Army quarters, just a few miles away, in a grubby run-down dump of a terraced house, provided by the military. I was a soldier, an NCO serving with the Royal Artillery Regiment, stationed at Lark Hill, a few miles to the south east of Stonehenge.

I had joined the Army in 1968 to escape the slow decline and despair of working night shifts in the remains of Lancashire's cotton mills. I knew in my heart that I was a writer, a poet, a spiritual man and my wife, Mary, seriously supported the dreams I had of one day becoming an author. In the meantime, I soldiered on to earn a living, studying poetry and classical literature in my spare time. We were there at Stonehenge on a cold Sunday in mid-December of the year 1972, seeking inspiration and insights into our uncertain destiny. It was raining as I placed my hands against the chill damp surface of those ancient stones.

I felt a sadness within and heard a silent voice speak my name: 'John….John, the world will know your name.'

There were tears in my eyes; how could that be, I wondered, it seemed hopeless. Then, from the near distance, I heard Mary call, 'John, you'll get wet, come and have a cup of tea.'

My parents had been to visit us some weeks previously in our shambolic residence, located in the middle of a crumbling red brick terrace. It looked like some deranged architect had designed a Salford slum and misplaced it amidst the wild rolling Wiltshire plains. Our house on Vimy Crescent sported a big hand-painted sign, 'You Got It, KEEP IT', placed there by me, as I had just about had it to the neck with door-to-door salesmen. Not only did the sign keep them away and, yes, it did work, it also helped my father locate our home. He recognised the attitude expressed in the warning on my door.

We had enjoyed a wonderful weekend with my parents, visiting Salisbury and going to see a concert by The Syd Lawrence Orchestra. It was my custom to keep in reasonably close contact with my mother and father. I was of the habit of calling them by public telephone once a week, usually on a Friday evening. Strangely, there had been no answer when I called on this last Friday, so I had tried again on the Saturday, but still no reply. On our way home to the cold comforts of our grim quarter, I decided to try calling again. Stopping my dark blue VW Beetle by the red telephone box at the end of our road, Mary and I both got out and went to call my mother and father.

I dialled the number, I heard the ring tone clearly, but still no one picked up and I was now concerned, as this had never happened before. After a few minutes of no reply, I replaced the handset and we left the telephone box. The door closed behind me and, as it did so, I glanced at my wife, Mary. She had a weird far-away look in her eyes and was suddenly pale.

'The door; it closed with a mighty boom. John, I know this is horrible, but your father is ill, he will not recover. John, your father is going to die.'

For a moment, we stood together silently in the rain, staring at that bright red telephone box as the enormity of what Mary had said slowly sank in.

18 Months Later:

Ejecting difficult drunks from a tough town local nightclub, deep inside the industrial north of England, was not exactly spiritually uplifting work. I threw out quite a few wannabe hard men, though, and some even put up a fight, but resistance was useless. I usually dumped them in the back alley, gently, of course. The year was 1974 and political correctness was unheard of; well, at least in my part of Manchester, anyway. It was a time when, if you were foolish enough to go looking for trouble, you didn't have to look far.

For a while, I acted as close protection to celebrities, working with, amongst others, Frankie Laine, the American singer, with hits such as 'High Noon'. He was a complete gentleman and so kind he needed only someone to get him through the crowds of adoring fans. Then there was Tommy Cooper; he was a big man, huge hands and it was always one bottle of gin before the show. He would stand behind the stage curtain, chuckling and swigging the stuff, then another after he had accepted his standing ovation. On his last night at the club, Tommy stuffed something in my dinner jacket pocket and said, 'Son, have a drink on me.' It was a tea bag.

Jack Jones, the American heartthrob crooner, was a really arrogant pain in the backside. He insisted on the bar closing as he sang. The way he performed; well, in my opinion, he would have been better with the bar doing loud trade. I was with Angelo Dundee, on protection, a quiet man who refused to meet the public. My job was to make sure they left him well alone, and they did. I had that knack of imparting the message to stay clear, without speaking a word. They called me 'Big John' because, at 5 foot 7 inches, I was the smallest of all the bouncers working in the club. In fact, Angelo signed his autograph for me: 'To John, quite big, Angelo Dundee'.

I'd been around a bit, served in The British Army as an NCO and won the Regimental Boxing championship at Middleweight.

I had even trained with the Special Air Services in winter warfare and was a veteran of Libya 1969, when Colonel Gaddaffi over-threw King Idris, then sent his troops to surround my battalion at RAF El Adam, miles inside the Sahara desert. But here I was, 25 years of age, going sweet nowhere. Life after the military was proving to be rather tougher than I had imagined, so while I looked for my next opportunity, I earned a living man-handling boozed-up losers and louts.

It was, at times, dangerous work and, on more than one occasion, I ended up in the accident and emergency unit, having my wounds stitched up. One night, a pair of half-baked idiots refused to leave the club; the cleaners swept up round them and, in the end, sent for the bouncers to move them out. I tried reasoning, but they just did not want to take my advice, so I suggested I carry them out gently. I mean, seriously, I did try, but the next thing I knew, I was wearing a glass pint-pot hat, with the jagged end sticking into my skull. Hot red blood squirted through my hair, running down my forehead dripping into my eyes.

I can still hear the man screaming as I lifted him through the fire-exit, face first, 'Yah. Ahhhhh! You've bust my bastard nose! Aaahhh!'

One of the cleaning staff ran and told my wife, Mary, who worked part-time behind the cocktail bar. I believe that when they advised that someone had attacked her husband, she replied, 'God help them.'

The wound I sustained that night required stitching at A&E, the crescent-shaped scar is still visible in my scalp and the blood ruined my dark blue velvet evening jacket.

It was the morning after another late night at 'Blightys', the night club where we worked, and my wife, Mary, was with me in our small rented flat, situated on the old road out of the town of Leigh, Lancashire. On the coffee table before me was yesterday's copy of The Daily Mirror. I was drinking a cup of hot black Nescafe, casually looking through the paper, when I saw a display advertisement that showed a man in uniform, underneath the heading: 'Join The Modern Prison Service'.

While serving in Germany with the British Army of The Rhine or BAOR, I had been the Regimental Provost Corporal. That job entailed me running the guard house and managing the day-to-day regime of soldiers serving short periods of imprisonment, locking them up, shouting orders, nothing too demanding. It was work that I had not particularly enjoyed but obviously someone in a position of authority had considered I was the man for the job. Maybe it was my natural ability to address adversaries in an appropriate uncompromising manner; well, one that was effective. That or the fact I was the undisputed boxing champion and looked like I meant business. As I stared at that advert, my mind went back to Germany and I believed I could do it, but what would Mary think, as she knew I wanted to be a writer and a poet, not a jailer.

My life had changed dramatically on the 15th of May 1973 as my father, Frank Sutton, who had been ill for a few months with leukaemia, passed away. Mary's vision outside the telephone box that dark December day, just months before, had been sadly correct. He was only 44 years of age, had been a Police CID Detective Inspector with a promising career, a wife, three grown children and, suddenly, he was gone. To help my mother cope with life, I had purchased my discharge from the army and assisted in the traumatic months that followed.

Move of house, change of dynamics, new way to manage day-to-day and all that follows the early death of the head of a family, and my father had been that and so much more. It was some weeks into June of 1973 when I first discovered he was not, in fact, dead but alive and well in the next dimension of life that we know as the world of spirit. My mother had called round to our flat to join us for the evening meal and was in the kitchen helping Mary, when I arrived home. As I walked in through the door, I looked in absolute amazement as I saw, sitting in a chair there in our back lounge, my father, exactly as he was in life.

Yet he could not be there; my mind instantly registered that thought and I said, 'What are you doing here, Dad?'

He was dressed in his traditional dark suit, white shirt and tie, with dark wavy hair and a subtle, slightly sardonic smile. In the next instant, he had disappeared. And yet, he was not gone; I knew he was watching over me and had returned to tell me that life was eternal, there is no death.

Over the next year or so, I would, on occasion, get a brief fleeting glimpse of my father's spirit, most frequently in places which were of some significance to him. In my mind, I would hear his voice, though he did not specifically guide or instruct me in any way; this was more of a reassuring few words, often no more than an inflection of my name, 'John,' spoken as only my dear father could, in a way that meant, without any doubt, 'Do that, boy, and you will get all you are asking for.'

You see, my father came from a long line of strict disciplinarians and he, like his own father and grandfather before him, was not a man to be messed with. So, just by the way I heard his spirit speak my name did I receive his directions from beyond the veil that we mistakenly call death.

With Mary by my side on our settee, I showed her the advert in The Daily Mirror and asked what she thought about me applying for a job as a Prison Officer. We had nothing, Mary and I, or just about next to nothing. The place we lived in was a one-bedroom rented flat that, in fact, constituted the lower half of a two-bedroom terraced property. I had a clapped-out old Triumph Herald car that was a faded shade of white and rust, though it ran; well, most of the time, at least.

We had been married four years on the 6th of August and had so far accumulated some mismatched second hand furniture, a stack of scratched, worn out 45 rpm records, a record player that sometimes worked, a faulty B/W television, a bad-tempered ankle-biter Jack Russell dog Mary had called Snowy and, apart from what we wore, that was about it. Mary worked full-time in a little antique shop I had helped my mother set up, called 'Then & Now Antiques', off the main shopping street in the town of Leigh. I had been offered more work at the nightclub, where

Mary also did some shifts behind the bar, but it was pointless, with absolutely no prospects whatsoever. As she read through the advertisement in the paper, I looked thoughtlessly across the room at our beat-up TV set. It was switched off, but in that instant, I saw something move and, there on the screen, appeared the face of my father and he was smiling.

'Give it a try, John' said Mary, without too much enthusiasm, and handed me back the paper. I immediately wrote my name and address on the form that accompanied the newspaper advert, placed it in an envelope and posted it to The Prison Service.

I waited for weeks before I received a response to my enquiry sent to The Prison Service and, when it came, I was more than a little daunted by the contents of the reply. They wanted not only a highly detailed application form completed, listing every employer I had ever worked for, along with written references from them, but also independent references from persons of good standing within the community. My army service record was 'Exemplary', which is as good as it can be; I had to forward proof of this, details of all my family, along with dates of birth. It seemed endless, but I persevered. In one part of the application, I had to write a short account of why I wanted the job of a Prison Officer; if they had seen my old banger outside, they would have known. But I wrote something meaningful about offering offenders hope for the future by setting a good example and, as I wrote, I realised that this was, for me, actually true.

In the army, I had been required to lock up the soldiers in the guard house but I had always empathised with them, putting myself in their place, much as in there but for fortune go I. In my short essay, I told of the many times I would speak with the soldiers and tell them to look ahead as this was just a passing moment in their young lives. There were, amongst the prisoners, those that felt suicidal. The military prison is a harsh regime indeed; to those in despair, I always gave time, explaining that what they were doing was taking it all far too seriously. In the years ahead, they would look back and laugh at this, so all they had to do was smile and accept that time would solve everything. I even sang them some silly songs; I knew lots of George Formby's music and would make even the most desperate laugh, as they could see that here was the notorious Regimental tough guy, making fun of the crazy system. Some had wives, who would come to the guard house asking to see their husbands, and while I could not authorise that, I would always take time to advise them that their loved one was well and in good spirits.

What I wrote must have done the trick because, when I sent the lengthy application form back, I quite quickly received a letter, calling me for a written examination or test, to be undertaken in offices on Southall Street in Manchester.

HMP Strangeways is a huge Victorian jail, built in 1868, and situated just outside the city centre of Manchester, adjoining Southall Street. The offices where I had to attend to take the tests were built into the massive sixteen-foot-high brick walls of the prison. Inside, a giant prison officer, wearing a black uniform, white shirt and a severe frown, guided me to a waiting room, where I joined around twenty other applicants. I had a good look at my fellow travellers and thought they appeared a pretty smart bunch; suits and ties were the order of the day and most looked the part. There were, if memory serves me well, two female recruits, while the rest were all men, varying in age from around 25 to 45 years.

We passed a few moments together, wished each other luck and were soon ushered into the examination room, where a huge bald-headed Prison Officer was acting as the adjudicator. I can clearly recall the Civil Service examination paper that all potential recruits to Her Majesty's Prison Service had to pass before they could be considered for interview. One of the multiple-choice questions was: What would you not use to measure a distance between two objects a) rope, b) elastic band, c) chain, d) wheel. There were many such questions and, within the first few minutes, I fathomed out that as this was a strictly timed test paper, so there had to be a catch. That catch was, to me, obvious; within the fifty or so questions, there were some that were so complex that answering them would require serious concentration and time. These seemed to jump off the paper at me as I looked at it and I am certain I was shown these by my late father, who had himself passed all the police promotion examinations first time, with top marks. Now it was my turn and I just sailed through all the questions that were easy; or at least, to me they were. Then, when I had done that, I went back to the difficult ones and took my time.

Following the series of written papers, all potential recruits were taken to a waiting room, while the staff marked the completed documents. After a short time, the giant Prison Officer with the frown came in and began reading out a list of names, saying as he read these, would the individual please proceed back to the examination room. My name was not on the list, so I stayed put, along with just a handful of others. We were the ones who had been successful. I had passed the written examination, no problem, and was told that same day, I would be required to attend for an interview and medical examination, on a date to be notified.

I can remember how excited I was, driving my clunking and banging Triumph Herald car home, to tell Mary the good news. Late that afternoon, in our rented flat, with Snowy the ankle-biter nibbling at my sock, I told Mary that I had passed the Civil Service examination and was now awaiting a date for interview, to be held at Strangeways Prison within the next month. Maybe I could get that job; no more late-night bar room brawls, dragging drunks out of a club and battling in the broken back streets. We both hoped so and went for a quiet drink to celebrate. As I passed Mary a glass of wine and proposed a toast to success, she seemed to hesitate.

'To your success as a writer, John,' she said as our glasses clinked together. I certainly shared her sentiments but wasn't too sure they were looking for poets telling stories at HMP Strangeways.

CHAPTER 3

THE CONDEMNED CELL

Within a few weeks, I had been notified of the date of the medical examination and interview, again at the offices set into the wall of Strangeways Jail on Southall Street in Manchester. Came the day, it was late October 1974, I was ready and feeling good. Wearing my navy-blue blazer, grey trousers, a white shirt and dark-striped tie, I looked like an ex-military man. It was how I imagined the selection board would expect a respectable off-duty Prison Officer to look, rather old school and slightly formal. My beat-up Triumph Herald got me there on time and I parked it just a few yards from the offices. The door in the wall of Strangeways Jail was opened by the same giant jailer, black uniform, white shirt and dark tie, only this time, he was quite friendly, even offering me a cup of tea. I just knew I would get this job.

Having first completed the medical and passed without question, I was directed back to the waiting room, where I introduced myself to the two other men seated there. One was a hefty, broad-shouldered guy in his early forties, who told me he had just sold his coal round as, following the new legislation banning household coal fires, his trade had all but vanished. His name was Joe and we exchanged stories about our cars. I had once owned an E-Type Jaguar when I mistakenly thought I was going to prosper. Joe loved motors and told me he had driven over from Oldham that day in his late 1950s Rolls Royce Silver Shadow. The other man was about five years older than me, in his thirties, and had been a salesman in a furniture store that had closed down. One thing we three had in common; we were all in need of employment.

The interview board was made up of middle-aged men; a Prison Governor, a Chief Prison Officer and a Senior Civil Servant. I can recall being asked what newspaper I read and they seemed to like the idea I took The Daily Telegraph and did the crossword. The questions were general, or so I thought; then the Chief Prison Officer looked at me in a certain way and said, 'How would you deal with being attacked by an angry prisoner?'

I could not stop myself from chuckling. 'No problem,' I replied, thinking of the countless wannabes I had ejected from that night-club. 'I was the Middleweight Boxing Champion in the Army,' I advised and they appeared well satisfied with that response.

When asked about my personal interests, I spoke of cross-country running, weight training in the gym and made absolutely no mention whatsoever of metaphysical poetry. I got the job.

The formal instructions on joining the staff training school at HMP Strangeways came to me in the post, within days of completing my successful interview. I was to start on Monday 6th January 1975 and report for duty at 08:00 hrs to the main gate. The actual training course at the prison would not commence until February, but I was to be employed within the jail on other duties, pending that time.

Strangeways Prison, from the outside, looks much like the exterior of a mediaeval castle; grim gothic towers with an unmistakeable air of menacing malevolence. Within the sixteen-foot-high brick walls, in excess of one thousand prisoners were held, with sentences from a few weeks to many years of imprisonment. Serving the Greater Manchester area, the prison had been used as a place of execution, where prisoners sentenced to death by the courts were taken to the gallows inside the jail and hung by the neck until they were dead. Then their bodies were buried within the grounds of the prison, as they were considered unsuitable for internment in a consecrated churchyard. This was one serious building, designed to impress and intimidate the people of Manchester.

In the early morning mist of that freezing January day, as I walked up to the front gate, I got the message intended: all hope abandon, ye who enter here. It was 07:55 when I knocked on the old oak and metal door set into the gate at Strangeways Jail, presenting my papers to a rough-looking, hooded-eyed, unsmiling jailer. I was pointed at a nicotine-tinged waiting room.

'In there,' he growled.

After about forty-five minutes sitting alone in that dingy, cold waiting room, I was startled from my silent meditations by a deep loud voice.

'Mr Sutton?' I was awake. 'I am the Principal Training Officer. Come with me, please.'

The way this man spoke indicated he meant business. He was of average height, black uniform with the two-pip insignia of a Principal Officer on his lapels and piercing eyes. I followed him through the inner metal gates, into the main forecourt of Strangeways, up some stone steps and through a large, vaulted corridor to another set of locked gates. He opened these with his keys and ushered me inside. Suddenly, I was in the very heart of Strangeways. This was the central rotunda; it was like the hub of a gigantic wheel with a huge glass-sided dome, and prison wings four landings in height branching out from here. It is panoptical in design so the staff can, from this central point, at any time see down all the wings that were identified by letters, starting at 'A' Wing down to 'E' Wing.

As I stood there, just a few yards from the cast iron circular central grid that was in the centre of the rotunda, I could see inmates of all shapes and sizes, dressed in blue and white striped shirts with grey trousers, walking around, supervised by uniformed prison staff. There was a strange smell to the place; at first, I could not quite identify what it was, like a mixture of carbolic soap and stale urine. Then it came to me; Strangeways Jail stank like a giant public lavatory.

'Mr Sutton, I want you to follow this Officer for the day and get a good look round the prison,' the Principal Training Officer instructed. 'I want to see you in my office on E3 landing at 4pm.'

I turned and tried to introduce myself to the indicated officer who, just a moment before, had been standing beside me, but now he was heading off in the direction of B Wing and I had to run to catch up.

The officer appeared to be ignoring me, so I attempted to get his attention.

'I'm John,' I ventured, 'first day.'

He stamped to a halt, turned to his left, faced me and tipped back his peaked uniform hat. He was heavy and tall, with long arms hanging down almost to his knees; this was one seriously ugly-looking jailer. His grey bushy eyebrows met in the middle of his lined and obviously battered Neanderthal face. Black dull eyes glared at me, like he was staring at a specimen, while his bulbous twisted nose pointed 20 degrees to the right.

'That's Vicious Vic,' he grumbled in a deep dark monotone, nodding towards the Principal Training Officer. 'He's one mean bastard. I'm Jack, stay by my side.'

With that, he lumbered off and I duly followed, down some iron stairs onto the ground floor of B Wing. As we walked, I saw, at either side of this landing, cells with strong painted wood and metal doors. Outside of each were red cards that had written on them the names and sentences of the prisoners locked inside. At the far end of B1 landing, Jack stopped and indicated I should wait. He grunted something and went off, opening a nearby cell and walking inside.

It was an opportunity for me to get a proper look at the interior of Strangeways and I tried peering into the end cell of this landing, putting my left eye to the small judas hole in the door. Inside, the cell looked empty; there were no cards on the front, so I assumed no inmates were locked in. There was something weird in there, though; I could see the far wall quite clearly one second and, the next, it was hazy, as if obscured by a translucent white mist. I also felt distinctly ill at ease; a clammy coldness almost crawled over me and, for no identifiable reason, I began to feel extremely sad. It was as If a deep emotional depression had clutched my soul and I felt tears forming in my eyes.

'Let's go!' shouted Jack the jailer and I was moving along the landing, back in control; whatever it was that had gripped me was gone. 'I did a hanging guard in there once,' said Jack in a menacing voice. 'You've just been looking into the old condemned cell.'

All morning, I followed Jack round the jail as he went from cell to cell, collecting inmates for legal visits that took place in another part of the prison. There were no airs and graces with the man and he just barked orders at the prisoners who, without question, jumped up and did exactly what he said. At one point, he had to call two prisoners off the exercise yard; there were perhaps two hundred or more inmates, all walking round in various stone-flagged circles, observing almost total silence. Prison staff stood at all corners and a Senior Officer was at the edge, with a Prison Guard Dog beside him, attached to a handler; he was clearly in control.

Jack had a brief word with this man, said something like, 'Legal visits,' and gave him a list of the names. Jack then climbed up onto the slightly raised platform next to the Senior Officer and gave the most deafening bellow I had ever experienced. In the Army, I had heard Regimental Sergeant Majors drilling the soldiers and they were loud, but this man was in a different class.

'EXERCISE HALT!' he boomed and it echoed round Manchester, as all two hundred or so inmates were instantly standing still. '794 Jones....274 Harrison,' he yelled and two prisoners left the yard, reporting to Jack the jailer.

At approximately 11:30am, Jack got all the inmates from the visiting room, physically searched their bodies one at a time, ordered them into a line and practically marched them back into the main prison, where he sent them, wing by wing, back to their cells. I was in awe of this man; all morning, no inmate had questioned his authority, all had done exactly as he directed. He never flinched; this was his job and Jack the jailer knew how to do it. I wondered if I would ever have the nerve to issue commands to prisoners the way he had and have all obey instantly, without hesitation.

Back inside the jail, I stood with Jack as he supervised the serving of the main meal of the day, which for many, took place from a series of hot-plates located on the ground floor, underneath the rotunda. I watched as hundreds of prisoners came along, one landing at a time, to collect their food on sectioned stainless steel metal trays. I was really surprised to see how well presented the meal was and it certainly appeared to be good wholesome food. Within ten minutes or so of starting, the serving of around a thousand main meals had been completed and the prisoners were back in their cells, locked away. Jack indicated that we should stand at the far edge of the main central rotunda, ready to make an exit for lunch. I had not thought what I might have for my meal and asked Jack what the staff did. He gave me a rather intimidating glare and, in his heavy Manchester accent, growled, 'Boddingtons.'

At the edge of the central rotunda in Strangeways Jail, there is the duty Principal Officer's unit, located in a wooden-framed office. To the front left of this hangs a huge polished brass bell. I was standing next to Jack the Jailer when the bell rang and, instantly, around a hundred prison staff stampeded forward in a rush to get out. I did my best to keep pace with my mentor but these jailers were like a herd of wild bulls rampaging en mass, heading for the main gate. It was within the gatehouse that all the keys for the prison cells were housed on wall-mounted boards. The staff coming in dropped a numbered brass tally into the slot and, out the other side, came the keys that matched their number.

I walked by Jack as he completed this process in reverse; keys into the slot, tally out and onto his stainless steel key chain that was fastened to his black leather belt. We turned right out of the main gate of the prison, the same way I had entered, then Jack walked just a few yards, turned right again up a few steps and opened a door leading into a short corridor that ended in steep steps down. I followed him, assuming that this was the right thing to do and was pleasantly surprised to find that this passageway led into what looked like a bar. Staff in uniform stood ordering drinks and I watched as Jack bought himself a pint of Boddingtons Bitter Beer and a pie. It seemed a good idea to get a drink, but not beer at this time of day, so I bought myself a glass of lemonade and tried one of the meat and potato pies; tasty it was, too. The place was really busy and I noticed that some of the jailers were putting quite a few pints away, mainly of the local brew, Boddingtons; the actual brewery was a sharp left at the bottom of the street, within staggering distance.

At approximately twenty past one, Jack came up to me and indicated it was time to go back into the prison. He collected his keys and we walked quietly through the open courtyard into the main corridor, where we joined all the other staff in a form of parade in ranks, one behind the other, military fashion. Silence fell on the gathered group of jailers as a grumpy-looking old man, wearing the insignia of a Chief Prison Officer, wobbled out; he was just about bursting his uniform at the seams. I recognised him as one of the boozers, quaffing numerous pints in the prison club bar, where I had been that lunchtime. He looked a little pissed to me, then in strange stentorian tones with a heavy Yorkshire accent, he addressed us.

'You've all seen't Governor's h'order 'bout security warning from't police, well check yer' cars, watch out fot' any suspicious, yer' know, packages, bloody IRA threats… Go on then.'

The staff were clearly accustomed to this routine, as they all turned left and walked into the main part of the prison, crossing the rotunda onto their respective wings and landings. Jack looked at me and, in an amused way, said, 'That was our number one Chief Prison Officer.'

I spent the afternoon following Jack the Jailer round the prison, as he went from wing to wing, landing to landing, cell to cell, collecting prisoners for visits. He first went to the main visiting room, where he was handed a list of inmates to collect and off we went, from one end of Strangeways jail to the other.

One prisoner he had to collect was working that afternoon in a unit Jack referred to as 'Mailbags'. We crossed through a long concrete tunnel that took us to a series of workshops; at the far top right, he opened a grey painted iron door and we stepped back a hundred years. There before me, sitting in row after row on hard wooden benches, were over a hundred prisoners, all silently sewing, by hand, Royal Mail Mailbags. They had long thin needles, threaded with what looked like string, and were supervised by Prison Officers, seated on huge raised platforms. It looked like a scene from a novel by Charles Dickens.

The Discipline Officer in charge of the shop acknowledged Jack and informally indicated he could call out the prisoner required for a visit.

'268 Thomas,' he boomed.

Instantly, a little scruffy man with thin dark greasy hair and nicotine brown broken teeth limped up to Jack and, in a wheedling tone that sent shivers down my spine, said, 'You're very kind, Sir, very, very kind.' All the way back to the visiting room, 268 Thomas kept wheedling on and on and on. 'You're kind. Sir, you are, very kind, very, very kind'.

We were about two hundred yards from the visiting rooms, when Jack stamped to a halt. I could sense the tension, but obviously 268 Thomas couldn't, as he was just about to utter yet another series of grovelling 'very, very kind, Sir,' remarks, when Jack slapped him on the side of the head. It was not a pole axe of a punch, more of a swipe; the kind one might have administered to a recalcitrant child in the days before corporal punishment became an offence.

268 Thomas did not react; he just looked at Jack. 'Very kind, Sir, you're very, very kind.'

Unbelievable as it seemed, that pitiful specimen of human life appeared to enjoy the attention he received, despite it consisting of a reasonably hard slap to the head.

Jack really had showed me the way round Strangeways and, at three-thirty, suggested we visit a place he called The Kardomah.

It was a kind of cafeteria, serving tea and coffee, located immediately to the left, in a room off the corridor leading to the main body of the jail. I thought it strange indeed that the refreshments were served to the staff by a prisoner, who accepted payment for the drinks and biscuits purchased. No one else seemed to think anything of this, so I got a black coffee and sat with Jack and a few other officers at a table, where the talk was all about football and George Best. I told Jack I had to be at the Principal Training Officer's office at 4pm and he agreed to take me there.

'Watch Vicious Vic, he's one mean bastard,' warned Jack.

Inside the prison training unit office, I was told to sit down and given a short but rather intimidating lecture by the Principal Officer. This mainly centred on what I may and may not disclose about what I would see and hear while on duty inside HM Prison Strangeways. I was, so Vicious Vic said, subjected to The Official Secrets Act and no part of my duties were to be discussed in any way whatsoever, with anyone outside these walls. In the event that I did speak of anything that happened within Strangeways Jail and it got back to the Governor or his senior staff, then I would be prosecuted under the Official Secrets Act and dismissed from the Prison Service.

Vicious Vic did have a sense of humour though. 'You can tell your wife where you work, but leave it at that,' he said and I honestly believed that he really did mean it.

I was then advised that, pending the start of the official training school programme, some four weeks hence, I was to report Monday to Friday on a daily basis at 08:00 to the Censors Office on I Wing in the Young Offenders unit. There, I would work under the close supervision of the senior staff and do as I was instructed. Vicious Vic omitted to say, 'Or Else!' but he really didn't need to. I could see it written all over his office wall.

CHAPTER 4

THREE MONKEYS

Within the walls of HMP Strangeways in 1974, there was a separate unit for offenders under the age of 21 years. This unit was housed in what had, at one time, been the female prison and it consisted of four wings, one of which held what they termed Young Offenders, aged 18 years to 21 years, and two wings that were for prisoners aged under 21 years of age, serving a Borstal sentence but awaiting allocation to a Borstal establishment. The design of this unit was similar to the main prison; a central rotunda with the wings G, H, I and K extending out four landings high, like the spokes of a wheel. My place of duty was in the mail censors' office on I Wing, inside two cells converted into an office.

I reported there at approximately 8am on Tuesday the 7th of January and was instantly made to feel most welcome by the obviously aged, bald, crumpled shirt and soup-stained tie-wearing Senior Officer in charge. He briefly explained what this job entailed and introduced me to his two members of staff, who grunted something unintelligible as I took the seat I was pointed at. The office itself was full of outdated, battered, dark wooden furnishings and it had a 1950s feel about it. There were a series of desks with pigeon-hole shelves above them that were allocated to each wing, so G Wing had its own desk and set of pigeon-hole shelves, as did H, I and K. The pigeon-holes were arranged by landing and sub-divided alphabetically, with each prisoner having a letter sheet listing incoming and outgoing mail. As the incoming mail for the inmates arrived in a huge mailbag sack, it was sorted between the staff and each letter was opened and briefly read to ensure it contained no contraband goods, drugs, threats to security or escape plans, etc. Then, it was placed into the correct pigeon-hole with the letter sheet annotated for onward transmission to the Discipline Officers staffing the landings, who then distributed the letters to the inmates. Outgoing mail was also read and anything untoward was struck through with a blue pencil and the letter sent back to the prisoner to rewrite, omitting the offending material. My job was to do exactly as the experienced staff did and censor both the incoming and outgoing mail.

It did not take me long to realise that the officers staffing the censors' unit had a jaundiced view of prisoners, coupled with a dark and somewhat disturbing sense of humour. I had been at the desk just over an hour and was sorting my pile of incoming mail into wing order, when I heard one of the staff start reading out loud from an incoming letter to a young prisoner.

'Listen this shit, sent to that thug, Dooley, the cleaner on K2, from his loving mother in Toxteth. 'Your dad's been sent to jail again, him and your Uncle Ted got five years each at Liverpool Crown Court for wounding that bastard who grassed him up for the burglary. He's in Walton. We went to see him on Saturday. Dad sends his love.' Dooley's older brother is on C Wing, doing twelve months, his mother has just done six months in HMP Styal for stabbing a neighbour. The whole bloody family's in and out of prison. I remember his father when he was on B Wing, doing three for robbing an off-licence; a right scruffy, arrogant scouse cunt, done more time than Big Ben. Hang the useless bastard lot of them and do society a favour'.

This was greeted with a form of mumbled agreement from the other staff I felt compelled to say something.

'Are perhaps the Dooley family from a socially disadvantaged background?' I ventured.

A form of growl rippled round the office, as all three of the prison officers turned and stared at me.

'No! they're a bunch of thieving, violent Irish gypos from fucking Toxteth!' the jailer who had read the extract from Dooley's mail shouted at me.

Instantly, I realised I had made a mistake and attempted to recover by expressing what I hoped was understanding.

'Oh, I see,' I said and went back to my stack of unopened mail.

Within moments, I heard a loud laugh from across the room.

'Polaroid Pussy!' shouted the jailer opposite me and passed a photograph to his colleague.

They were chuckling about this and, seeing that I was interested, held it up for me to see. The rather grainy black and white Polaroid picture showed a completely naked young woman with her right foot on a chair, pulling open the petals of her pudenda. The officer explained that these sort of photographs often came in, as the girlfriends of inmates sent them to keep their boyfriends amused. It certainly entertained the censors' staff, who appeared to get some strange vicarious pleasure from peering at that 'Polaroid Pussy'.

'Call him up and warn him,' said the Senior Officer, handing a sheet of A4 paper to the staff.

It was 4pm in the censors' office when the young prisoner whose girlfriend had sent in the naked Polaroid photograph of herself appeared. He had been summoned to the unit to be given an official warning that he may not receive such items as Polaroid photographs in the mail and that it was being destroyed. I quickly perceived that, while this was absolutely correct and strictly according to the rules, it was also being used by the staff as a form of amusement. To start with, the young prisoner had no idea why he had been sent for; he looked acutely embarrassed as he was shown the Polaroid picture of his girlfriend exposing herself.

'You are not permitted to receive such items in the mail, do you understand?' Then came the turn of the screw. 'It looks like it's been well battered to me and ask yourself this, boy, who took the photograph?...ha ha ha.'

With that, the censor's officer ripped the Polaroid snapshot into pieces and threw them in the green metal wastepaper bin. The prisoner was blushing bright red as he made a hurried exit from the office, to peals of resounding laughter from the staff.

Back home in our little rented one-bedroom flat on St. Helens Road in Leigh, Lancashire, Mary was waiting to tell me some really weird news. That day, she and my mother had been to see a local psychic-medium called Mrs Lillian Hill, for what she told me was a clairvoyant reading, rather like fortune-telling. I had heard of Mrs Hill before; she was well known in the area for helping the police with difficult cases and I believe that, at one point, my late father had spoken to her in his capacity as a Detective Inspector. It seemed that Mary had been persuaded to have a psychic consultation with this lady by my mother, who had also paid for her own reading, as well as Mary's.

OK, I thought, as Mary appeared quite full of this news, let's hear it. What Mary told me Mrs Hill said to her was not what I would call good news; there were no predictions of us winning a fortune on the football pools or anything even remotely like that. It was, Mary said, a truly mysterious message that both she and my mother had been given.

'It was all about you, John,' Mary explained. 'I could hear what Mrs Hill said to your mum and she told her that one of her two boys was going to be famous and everyone would know his name. Your mother insisted that this would be her younger son, Martin, who had recently joined the police, but Mrs Hill would not have that. She said it was the eldest son and he would do many amazing, wonderful things and all would hear about him.

'Then I went in and Mrs Hill did not know that your mother and I were connected; she just looked at me in a really odd way and told me of a man who would try and try and try again and again and again to be a success. 'He is climbing a golden ladder,' she told me, then explained how this man would suffer at the hands of others, how angry men would attack him, terrible troubles, she said, but he would climb up to prominence. But she said this man was destined to be knocked down, after getting to a certain level, by liars full of hate, that people would fear him, but he would start again, then once more gain a level of success, only to be knocked off the ladder, time after time after time.

'John, she told me you were that man and it was going to be one terribly tough struggle but you, John, would get there in the end, as she said you simply never give in and you climb to the top of that golden ladder. But, John, as she said this, Mrs Hill looked at me with tears in her eyes. John, she was crying for us'.

So that really cheered me up. I was just starting work in the Prison Service and it seemed, according to the psychic predictions of Mrs Hill, that no matter how hard I tried, my destiny was to endure a series of traumatic failures.

The training school at Strangeways Jail started for me at the end of January 1975. There were six of us in the group; I had the key to the classroom, as Vicious Vic the Principal Officer in charge decided I had to show them round and assume the role of team leader. As a kind of joke, Joe, the ex-coalman I met at the interview, called me Moses. Each day, for the next month, we would report for duty at 7am and shadow the duties of nominated Discipline Officers on the various wings and landings. This would be followed by physical training in the prison's gymnasium, where the Officer Training instructors would ensure that we were fit for the job.

I was myself reasonably athletic but a few of the other new recruits were clearly not and, after one particularly rigorous series of exercises involving running on the spot and jumping over hurdles, two of them collapsed. They were warned, as were we all, that if we failed the final fitness test, then our planned progress to the Staff Training School would be cancelled and our career in the Prison Service terminated.

On the landings each morning at 7am, I watched as, down below, the duty Principal Officer rang the big brass bell for unlock and, round the wings, echoed the sounds of jailers shouting, 'Slop Out!' There were no toilet facilities within the cells; the inmates had to use plastic pots and buckets that they filled during the time they were locked in, usually from around 7pm to unlock at 7am.

So, for twelve consecutive hours, the prisoners had no access to the toilets. Not that there were many WC units; on E3 Landing, where I was, there were just four open WC units with eight toilets, separate urinals and slop basins, to serve a total of approximately one hundred and fifty prisoners. The cells measured 12' X 8' and, due to lack of accommodation, they frequently held three inmates. At unlock, these prisoners had been banged up for at the least ten hours and the smell was quite overpowering. The inmates did not restrict themselves to using their pots to excrete into, as a night with three pots full of steaming crap and urine would have been unbearable.

To circumvent the loaded potty situation, the standard trick was to get the excrement out of the crowded cell. This was not as easy as one might think; the method used was for the prisoner to take sheets of newspaper, place these on the floor of the cell and defecate into that. Then, the newspaper with contents would be folded up into a bundle and thrown out of the cell's window, through the bars, usually landing on the ground outside the cell block. They called these bundles of human excrement 'Shit Parcels'. The stench was quite horrendous and it drifted through the jail, causing it to smell like a very dirty public lavatory.

Strangeways Jail held many inmates serving prison sentences for violent offences, such as wounding with intent, grievous bodily harm, assaulting with a deadly weapon, etc. It was therefore something of a surprise to me when I saw the Discipline Officers on the landings distributing razor blades, one to each inmate. These were not sealed unit razors, these were actual blades that the inmates placed in their issue metal razors to shave with. To me, it seemed like a crazy thing to do and I asked the experienced Officer I was shadowing if there had been many incidents involving attacks with these blades.

He motioned me to follow him down the landing a few yards, where he stepped into the WC Recess and lit a hand-made roll-up cigarette. Staff were not allowed to smoke on duty and he indicated I should watch out for any senior officers approaching, then pushed back his hat, took a long drag on his fag and said, 'Yeah, they cut each other from time to time, worst I saw was some nutcase split a blade into small pieces and hammered them into one of the wooden toilet seats, the poor bastard that sat on that had his backside cut up to buggery.'

After all the inmates on the landing had been down and collected their breakfasts, which they carried back to the cells and ate inside, they were locked in. The staff called this banging them up, which they made to look incredibly easy. In fact, most of the inmates closed the cell doors themselves. There then followed a detailed counting of all prisoners, now secured into their cells. This involved the discipline staff going from cell to cell, looking in through the small judas spy-hole, observing the inmates inside and counting them down each side of the landing. The two totals were then given to the most senior officer on the landing, who reported them to the Wing Principal Officer, by shouting the number down. All round the jail could be heard the sound of officers reporting their numbers: '148 on the threes,' etc. It was a rather noisy but efficient process, completed from unlock, slop out, through breakfast and bang up within 45 minutes.

Outside the main walls of the prison, there was located, some few hundred yards across open land, a series of buildings that formed part of HMP Strangeways. These buildings consisted of a number of flats used by single or married officers and, on the ground floor, there was an Officers' Mess room that served meals. Joe the ex-=coalman was particularly pleased with the food served there and referred to the early sausage, bacon, egg and beans with fried bread and toast as his bargain breakfast.

The meals were at a nominal cost and looked really good value. In fact, I was tempted to eat there myself until I saw that, apart from one Prison Officer in control, all the rest of the staff in there were prisoners. The cooks were inmates, the cleaners were prisoners, there were no civilian employees whatsoever in the Officers' Mess at Strangeways. Now I had seen where these inmates lived, in absolute squalor, three to a cell, banged up all night and no doubt hurling shit parcels out of their cells. Well, I just couldn't eat the food.

In time, I would discover that my judgement was absolutely correct but, for now, all I had was a sense of unease about allowing inmates that I would be locking up to prepare and serve me food. So, while Joe and the others tucked in to their substantial breakfasts, I sat in the lounge next to the dining area, reading my newspaper and drinking black coffee.

Each day, the six of us on the new recruits' training programme were given a specific unit of the prison to visit and observe how it functioned. We were required to make extensive notes and present these to Vicious Vic, the Principal Training Officer, on Friday evenings.

One particular day, I was scheduled to attend at the bath house or shower unit and watch what happened as the prisoners were processed through their weekly wash. Located on E1 Landing, the showers had been built into a series of converted cells, tiled in grubby white and with non-slip corrugated dark tile flooring. Next to the bath house was a cell containing clothing; this was where the inmates exchanged their underclothes and shirts, on a weekly basis.

The officer in charge seemed less than happy to have me with him and hardly spoke a word. He looked a surly individual, Brylcreemed dark hair, late forties, protruding belly, hat on the back of his head and a mean sneer on his face. I tried asking interesting questions but he just glared at me, stirred his pint pot of tea and pointed at the showers. I assumed he meant go in and have a look, so I did and made notes about exactly how many showers there were, how these were sited open plan with rough distances; if Vicious Vic wanted observations, he was going to get them.

I was just scribbling details of the clothing exchange unit, when the first batch of inmates came along, escorted by a Prison Officer, who reported the exact number to the bath house officer. And then all hell broke loose.

There had been quite a lot of pushing and shoving in the queue of prisoners waiting in line to use the showers. It appeared that one of them had attempted to walk to the front, where he had met with some serious resistance from the huge inmate, whose place he was trying to take. I did not see exactly what happened but heard the blood-curdling scream of the would-be queue jumper, who was now lying on the floor, holding his head and dripping gore from a savage wound to his face.

Quite how he had been cut was uncertain but the man that did it was on top of him, pummelling the top of his head with both fists. I heard a loud bell ringing; the two staff had pressed the alarm button. They were in that battle together, heaving and pulling with all their might, attempting to get the crazed aggressor off the injured inmate. Blood was splattering all over the place and I watched in astonishment as the jailers began to throttle the massive mad prisoner, who was making a horrible gasping gurgling sounds, fighting for breath.

Within less than a minute, the landing was full of uniformed jailers. They just snatched the big battling inmate up off the floor and ran him, shoulder high, off the wing. It was a practiced performance and one that, as a former bouncer in a tough nightclub, really impressed me. These guys knew how to do the business, no messing about, in and sorted before the man had time to think.

The wounded prisoner, who was not just badly cut but was also missing chunks of his hair, where the wild man of Strangeways had torn handfuls out, was slumped against the bath house wall. He looked a right mess and was, from what I could see of his face, fortunate not to have lost his right eye. Hospital Officers in white tunics took him away for treatment in the main clinic. This was certainly going to make some interesting reading for Vicious Vic, I thought, as I made mental notes. The surly Brylcreemed officer in charge of the showers gave me a suspicious look.

'You saw fuck all, understand, nothing. Three Monkeys, You Got That!' He wasn't joking; I could see the anger in his eyes and decided there must be a good reason. Thinking about what he had said for a moment, it became rather obvious. This was Strangeways; hear no evil, see no evil, speak no evil.

CHAPTER 5

PRISON STAFF COLLEGE

The initial month of training at HMP Strangeways, under the watchful eyes of Vicious Vic, was almost over and all six of us in the group were about to discover if we had passed the course. If we had, then we were to set off for the Prison Staff Training College at Leyhill, near Bristol. But before we were dispatched, there was the final interview with the Principal Training Officer, during which we would be advised if we had been successful. Not one of us was looking forward to this.

For the last time on the Friday, we all handed in our notebooks and, in return, Vicious Vic gave us a time to report to his office during the following Monday. Being the appointed team leader, or Moses as they all insisted on calling me, I would be the first. As I handed in my notes for the final week, I saw something I had not noticed before flicker across the face of Vicious Vic. It was a dark momentary, somewhat sinister, sardonic smile and it sent shivers down my spine.

'Mr Sutton,' he said in a crisp authoritarian tone, '9am Monday in this office and be aware, this for you is not all good news'.

I had the weekend to ponder on that veiled threat. How kind of him, I thought, as I handed back the classroom key, trying to remain calm. I had spent four weeks experiencing the mysteries of Strangeways and had done my best to note and understand how the many various departments that made up the prison worked. I needed this job; Mary and I were relying on it to enable us to make proper plans for our future. We had been married approaching five years and it was time we made some progress.

That night, back home in our rather run-down rented flat, I said nothing about the training officer's comment to my wife; one of us worrying was quite enough.

Late February 1975, it was Monday morning, a little before 7am and the mist drifting off the nearby river Irwell crept silently up Southall Street, curling round the vast oak and iron gates of Strangeways. Grim-faced jailers, in dark blue and black uniform overcoats, pushed past me, joining a long grumbling queue to collect their keys. The huge old metal bars of the inner gate swung open, allowing the staff in, then swiftly closed, clanging and banging as they no doubt had done for over a century.

Inside the prison, I stood watching the inmates shuffling along the landings, down the metal stairs, to collect their porridge, then back up into overcrowded cells. The jail echoed with shouts of 'Slop Out!' 'Bang Up!' as heavy doors slammed shut and the by now familiar stench of stale urine mixed with excrement filled the almost malevolent morning air.

I was waiting for the Duty Principal Officer to ring the big brass bell for staff break time, when my mentor, Jack the Jailer, walked across the central iron grid of the rotunda and came up to me.

'Good luck,' he said in his gruff Manchester accent. 'Staff College next, watch out for the gym instructors, really mean bastards.'

The central bell rang twice and, before I had chance to say thanks, Jack was gone. I saw him disappearing into a scrum of jailers, key chains jangling, hats wobbling on the backs of their heads, as they sped off for a bargain breakfast in the officers' mess.

At 8am in the prison's Kardomah snack bar, I sat with my fellow trainee prison officers and discussed what potentially awaited us that day. We each were scheduled a thirty-minute final interview with Vicious Vic, the Principal Training Officer. He had advised all of us that, if our work during the initial four weeks as potential prison officers did not meet an acceptable standard, then that would be the end of our careers in The Prison Service.

Joe, the ex-coalman, looked reasonably confident. I was less certain, wondering what on earth I had done to warrant a caution to expect something less than good news. I didn't have long to wait, as I was the first into the firing line at 9am, less than an hour away. The physical training tests had been passed, some with greater ease than others, but all of us had made at least an acceptable grade. Our notebooks, all signed and dated by the senior staff in charge of the units we had observed within Strangeways, were completed and with the Training Officer. All that remained to be done was for Vicious Vic to sign us off as having completed the initial month of training and we would be cleared for the next phase at the Prison Officers' Training College.

'Mr Sutton, sit down, please,' said the Principal Training Officer, with a slight edge to his curt authoritarian voice. 'I told you on Friday that this was not all good news and it isn't.'

I could see that sinister half-smile forming and a sense of trepidation gripped me by the throat, with fingers of cold steel.

'I was considering recommending you for accelerated promotion, as your written work has been consistently of a high standard. However, I have been watching you with the other members of the team, the team you were supposed to be leading, Mr Sutton.'

Slowly, the icy grip of terror eased and I could breath. Accelerated promotion? I wondered what he meant.

'Too relaxed, Mr Sutton. You did not take command, did you? This is a disciplined service and what I am looking for are leaders. Your work was of the highest standard, all your reports are excellent, but I am not recommending you for rapid promotion, as you did not assume strict control of your team'.

That was it; I was found wanting for failing to order my fellow trainee prison officers about. It had never really occurred to me to give them direct instructions. I just organised the meetings and classroom discussions, according to our rota.

'Mr Sutton, I have put my recommendations in writing to the Governor in charge of the Prison Staff College, and you are being closely observed. Congratulations on passing the initial training course.'

With that, Vicious Vic stood up and shook my hand. I had done it and all the worrying that last few days had been about nothing. I could hardly wait to get home and tell my wife, Mary.

The Prison Staff Training College was located in a converted manor house, within a few hundred yards of Leyhill Open Prison, in south Gloucestershire. On a gray cold Monday in March 1975, I drove down there in my battered old Triumph Herald. It was over 160 miles with no heater in the car; I had a rather grubby tartan blanket wrapped round my body that helped keep me warm, but my feet were freezing cold. The entrance to the college was a welcome, if somewhat imposing, sight; huge stone blocks supporting heavy ornate iron gates, leading into a winding tree-lined driveway.

I drove on some few hundred yards or so and, around a sharp right bend, saw before me the rather magnificent old country mansion house that was now the Prison Staff Training College. This huge pile had obviously been a residence of some import in times past. I parked the Triumph, lifted the case Mary had packed for me and headed to the arched hallway, through stout oak and iron doors. Inside, all that was missing were a few suits of armour and stag's head hunting trophies for the walls. There was a great wide wooden staircase, long stained-glass windows, a vaulted ceiling and a big man in Prison Officers' uniform, looking down at me. He didn't speak, just pointed to a door that had a sign on that read 'Registration'.

Joe the ex-coalman was there and we organised a meeting of our group from Strangeways Jail. Everyone seemed in reasonably good spirits, though we all felt this was a seriously spooky place, with its long oak-panelled corridors and shifting shadows. On registration, we had each been allocated a shared barrack-block-style bedroom within the main house and placed into units of twenty other new recruits. The course started the following morning at 9am, with a formal parade at the side of the building, somewhat like being back in the Army, I thought, as we formed ourselves into three ranks, one behind the other.

Our group instructor was a somewhat sanguine Principal Officer in his late forties, who optimistically enthused about life inside the walls of Her Majesty's Prisons. He had, he informed us, served in many: Wandsworth, Pentonville, Wormwood Scrubs, etc. Happy days. We had to keep notes and pay attention, he advised, as each formal lesson we received would be part of a written examination, to be taken weekly. To fail any of these examinations would result in automatic removal from the college and the end of any idea of a career as a jailer.

In the college, I met a hefty former policeman from Leeds, named Paul C. and I quickly discovered that we shared a common interest; beer. As I said, the college house was located some few hundred yards from Leyhill Open Prison and, within the grounds, there was a working farm and a Prison Officers' Club. Paul and I decided one night to visit this club and share some tall stories, over a few pints of the local brew. The way to this club was down the long winding driveway, to the road, turn right, four hundred yards or so, turn right into HMP Leyhill and there was the club.

Now, I did enjoy a beer or three, but my new buddy, Paul, liked it a lot more than me, so much so that, by the time it came to closing, he was extremely unsteady and in no mood to walk all the way back to the college, down the long dark road. Paul would, so he said, take a more direct route through the farm fields of Leyhill Open Prison and into the grounds of the mansion house, where we were resident. Nothing I said could dissuade him from this idea, so I wished him good luck and watched in wonder as he staggered off into the unknown darkness of a farmyard and fields.

It was 9am the following morning and, as usual, we trainee prison officers were standing on parade at the side of the house. I could hear some serious muttering in the ranks to my left and, when I looked across, I saw Paul C. was the centre of attention, as people were pointing at him. There was also a really horrible pungent stink coming from somewhere and that somewhere was the man himself. Looking at Paul, I could see he appeared even more of a shambolic mess than he usually looked; his jacket was smeared with filth, as were his trousers, and all down his side something dark and smelly clung to his clothing. The stench was drifting all round the parade ground and the Principal Officer taking the parade rapidly identified the odour

'Who has been in the pigsty?' he asked, looking directly at Mr Paul C.

I spoke to Paul at lunchtime that day and he explained what had happened. It seemed that, between the prison club at HMP Leyhill and the grounds of the college, there was an enclosed area known as a pigsty, but at the time Paul did not know this. In the darkness, under the heady influence of numerous pints of best bitter, he had made a bold and seriously mistaken assumption that he could climb the wooden fence enclosing the sty and cross to the other side. It seems the ground underfoot in said sty was somewhat slippery so that, as Paul jumped down from the fence, he slithered and fell, rolling over into a pile of what is commonly known as pig shit. Further falls had followed as Paul attempted to extricate himself from this revolting mire, which had resulted in his clothing being almost completely coated in pig muck.

On finally arriving back in the dormitory, where he was sleeping alongside three other new recruits, he had created mayhem. It seems he had staggered in and collapsed on his bed, covering the sheets in shit and filth, with the overpowering pong of pig muck making the bedroom virtually uninhabitable. Paul told me that no one in his group was speaking to him and the Governor of the training college had ordered a meeting later that day.

The training college course consisted of various specific segments, aimed at preparing us new recruits for the difficult task of maintaining good order and discipline within the various regimes that, in total, constituted Her Majesty's Prisons. We were training to be what the service termed Discipline Officers. Throughout the two months we were in the residential college, there were numerous rather obvious psychological tests taking place. Role-playing exercises had us taking part in scenarios during which, it was clear to me, our potential for prejudice was being tested.

There were also some rough and tumble encounters, organised by the Physical Training Staff, that required many of the trainee officers to engage in what amounted to violent combat for the first time. We were shown how to apply various restraints against the will of a powerful inmate. I frequently was selected to role-play the inmate and I had to resist. I recall one rather large trainee officer attempting to place me in a strangle hold; he just could not do it, despite having three others hold me down. In the end, he told the PT staff that it was not possible to apply that hold, as it simply had no effect. Thanks a lot, I thought, as the extremely fit and strong Physical Training Instructor came across, grabbed hold of my neck and half bloody killed me.

'That's how you do it,' he said.

I recalled the words of warning I had been given by Jack the Jailer: 'Beware the PT staff, they are total bastards'. He wasn't wrong and they were strong with it.

One really interesting lecture was on the history of The Prison Service and included details of how the various terms used in the jails had developed. During the Victorian era, when many jails such as Strangeways, Wormwood Scrubs, Pentonville, Wandsworth, Walton, etc. were built, the courts often sentenced inmates to what was termed hard labour. This punishment involved prisoners undertaking various arduous but non-productive physical tasks, such as walking on a treadmill that went endlessly round and round or turning a crank. The crank was a device that had a handle, much like an old-fashioned clothing mangle, which the prisoner had to turn over 14,000 times a day and the resistance was controlled by a screw at the top of the crank. So, if the jailer tightened the screw, it would make it more difficult for the inmate to turn the handle. That was, we were advised, how Prison Officers came to be known as 'Screws'.

The term 'doing your bird' derived from the period an inmate must be serving to be afforded the privilege of keeping a pet bird within their cell. 'Porridge' was prison slang for the period spent inside prison when, each morning, porridge oats were part of the breakfast meal.

During the final weeks of the course, we were given a brief lecture by a representative of The Prison Officers' Association, in which it was explained to us that, while as newly-recruited staff, we could join until we became substantiated i.e. had passed the course and our probationary period, we would not be full members of the POA. This seemed a little strange to me, as the idea of any trade union was to protect the interests of its members and, if the POA did not actually offer full protection to new staff, what was the point?

But at that stage of my involvement with the Prison Service, I did not feel it would help if I started asking too many difficult questions. We were all invited to join the POA and, as it was the only way one could reasonably get some form of representation, everyone, including myself, did so. We were advised that each prison had its own POA committee and that the elected officers were there to help and advise all members. The subs were not exorbitant and they were payable monthly by direct deduction.

On Fridays, we had the written examinations. These were formal tests of our knowledge of the content of the course that we had been taught during the previous weeks. By week six, I had recorded 100% all the way through and I could see the Principal Officer Instructor giving me some serious stares as he handed out the results each week. Following the examinations, we were all allowed home to report back for first parade, Monday morning. At the end of week six, we had been asked to complete a detailed submission, stating the name of the establishment we would like to be posted to, on completion of our training.

I took my form home with me and, over the weekend, discussed the possibilities with Mary, as she would be with me on this serious decision that would affect our lives for a long time ahead. I had in my mind the idea that I would like to work with young offenders, as I seriously believed I could potentially have a positive influence on them. I really believed that, then.

So, having spoken with Mary, I completed the document and listed as my first choice a Borstal for young offenders in the South

West of England. It seemed to offer the kind of challenge I was looking for in a career. As strange as it may seem now, at the time, I did believe I could make a positive difference and I was determined to do my best.

Back at the Prison Staff Training College, the course was nearing its end and we were called in to the lecture hall, to be given a talk by the Chief Prison Officer in charge of the staff. He was a powerfully-built man in his mid-fifties, with close-cropped gray hair and a deep resonating voice. He told us all that he had been in the Prison Service for over thirty years and now we were here, about to start our careers, heading towards what he said was to be the great prize at the end, a Government Pension. I had honestly never thought at all, for one single minute, about an old age pension. I was twenty-five years of age; I wanted to do something with my life, not fill in time to draw a pension. I had to hand it to this Chief Officer; he had just about achieved his goal. But what kind of a dismal prospect was this; no talk of doing good, no mention of helping unfortunate inmates, just bang 'em up and, after thirty years, get that glorious pension. Strange as it seems, that man was right.

My buddy on the course, Paul C., had survived his meeting with the Governor of the college. It seemed he was told in no uncertain terms that any more drunken antics and he was out on his ear. Paul told me he had been asked if he had a drinking problem, to which he assured me he replied that indeed he had; it was too expensive, he could not afford it. How he got away with that, having wrecked his dormitory with pig shit, is a mystery to me. Paul was a truly unconventional character and we were destined to be friends.

On the final day of the course, we were all congratulated by our Principal Training Officer and handed a sealed brown envelope that contained the details of our postings. I was really looking forward to this, working with young offenders, helping them to get back on track and live decent hard-working lives; it really did seem to me to be a worthwhile job. I opened the envelope, full of hope and expectation. Inside, I saw these words: HMP Wormwood Scrubs, Du Cane Road, London W12. The biggest adult male prison in Europe and I was going there as a Discipline Officer, to patrol the landings.

That night, when I arrived home and told Mary, she just shook her head and looked at me. 'You've certainly done it this time, John.'

CHAPTER 6

HMP WORMWOOD SCRUBS

London, the Big Smoke, as they call it, population of around eight million. Expensive place to live but I was not too concerned, as the Prison Service provided free housing for staff, so I fully expected that, soon, Mary and I would be relocating to a quarter. Suitcase in the boot, I kissed my wife farewell and drove off to start a new phase of life, two hundred or so miles south. My old Triumph Herald got me there, sixty miles an hour, nice and steady down the M6 motorway. And so it was that one sunny afternoon in the middle of May 1975, I presented myself at the famous iconic gates of Her Majesty's Prison Wormwood Scrubs. The massive twin towers that form the gatehouse were frequently featured on television cops and robbers series such, as 'No Hiding Place' and in many feature films, like 'Billy Liar'. The image of HMP Wormwood Scrubs was absolutely synonymous with what one associated with a British Prison. The white and brown brick façade of the two towers, with oval plaster relief images depicting Victorian prison reformers Elizabeth Fry and John Howard, create an instantly identifiable entrance. The mighty oak and iron doors have a smaller gate set into them to the right side and it was at this that I knocked, wondering just what wonders awaited within.

HMP Wormwood Scrubs is named after the open grassland area on which it was built in 1874 and completed in 1891. The jail was designed by Sir Edmund Du Cane, after whom the adjoining road is named. It has a sixteen-foot-high brick wall, enclosing a series of four separate cell blocks, each with four long landings of cells. I stood just inside the main gate and presented my documents, instructing me to report for duty to the senior officer, who peered at me from behind a partitioned glass screen, as if I was a seriously suspicious individual.

'Wait over there,' he grunted at me, pointing to a dark corner on the opposite side of the entrance.

I was there for what seemed like hours and I began to feel a little uneasy standing there; no one spoke to me. The atmosphere was oppressive, still and sullenly silent, but then this was a jail, a one-hundred-year-old prison, so it should create a sense of trepidation. I was becoming concerned that they had forgotten about me when a surly old jailer with a soup-stained jacket came over and stared at me.

'You Sutton, ya come with me.' He spoke with a thick Glaswegian accent and reeked of tobacco.

'Nice place you have here,' I ventured but answer came there none.

The Principal Officer in charge of training at HMP Wormwood Scrubs had a unit inside a large, relatively modern office block, located to the right of the main gates. I was led into the building, where my soup-stained Scottish guide silently pointed at a door, indicating that was where I was to go. Inside, to my great delight, I saw sitting at the far end of the room, none other than my boozing buddy from the staff college, Mr Paul C. We exchanged observations about our mutual fate and agreed that we needed to test the supply of beer at our earliest opportunity. Paul told me he had applied to be posted to HMP Liverpool, as that was where he intended to set up home with his new wife. He did not appear too enthusiastic about being a jailer in The Scrubs, some two hundred miles or so south of his chosen posting. Time passed and a number of other new staff arrived; I recognised them from the college. In total, there were six of us posted into the prison as Discipline Officers. It was, by now, around 2pm in the afternoon and, so far, I had no idea where I would be spending the night.

Principal Officer M, the training officer, was tall, thin and had a weird way of staring right through you, as if he could see your soul and didn't much care for what he was looking at. He explained we would spend a period on an introduction course to familiarise us with the workings and layout of the prison. For the next two weeks, we were to move around the jail, experiencing all the different units. He said that Wormwood Scrubs had various regimes, such as a Borstal Allocation Unit, a Young Offenders Unit, a Long-Term Prisoners wing, a Local Prison wing for inmates sentenced by the London courts, a hospital wing, a High-Security Segregation Unit and numerous workshops.

We were advised that, for the first twelve months of our service, we would be on probation and reports on our conduct would be made by senior staff and passed to him. On completion of the initial introduction period, we would each be allocated a post within one of the wings or units of the prison. But the first thing we needed was our uniforms; we had all been measured for these at the college and they were now awaiting us in the store, which is where we were taken.

Loaded down with two full prison uniforms, a heavy-duty all-weather jacket, four nylon shirts, a couple of navy blue clip-on ties, a leather belt, a long stainless steel keychain, a wooden truncheon, a metal whistle and two Prison Officer caps, we all stood in a semi-circle, like contestants in a double-or-drop competition. It was now fast approaching 5pm and still we had no advice on where we would be staying. Some of the new staff were actually from London and had accommodation. Paul and I had no idea where we were to be accommodated. I had imagined that, rather like the Army, the Prison Service would have a form of barrack block for staff, but they didn't. The training officer advised that what he did have was a list of local residents who took in lodgers and they particularly favoured prison staff, as their presence made them feel safe. I looked at Paul and an image of him staggering drunkenly into some poor old woman's house covered in pig shit came to my mind; how safe would that make one feel?

Principal Officer M handed me a slip of paper with a name

and address on. He advised that this was reasonably close to the prison, on Carlisle Avenue at the end of Du Cane Road, off Western Avenue, and the elderly couple were expecting me. Paul was given a similar note with an address and directions, so off we went to our respective lodgings, with instructions to return the following morning at 9am, dressed in uniform. I stuck all the uniform bits into the back seat of the Triumph and set off to make the acquaintance of the people in the house on Carlisle Avenue.

The old lady who opened the door to me was a really nice genteel person, silver-white hair and softly spoken. She had a proper look at me and then invited me into her sitting room, where she introduced me to her older brother. He was a gentle soul, rather infirm and in his early eighties. We had a brief talk and he told me he had worked for over forty years as a train driver. My room was a double bedroom at the front of the house; the old lady had the single room next door and her brother the double room at the back of the house, next to the bathroom. It seemed nice and neat, a small chest of drawers, a wardrobe, double bed and I could see that this would be fine for a few weeks, till I could arrange for a Prison Service house and bring Mary to join me. But I felt something that first night, alone in the room on Carlisle Avenue; I felt lonely. This was not my home, this was London, this was a big city and what exactly awaited me within the walls of Wormwood Scrubs jail?

I did not sleep at all well that night, despite being exhausted from the long drive down and all the nervous tension involved in entering that grim old prison. Thoughts of Mary, hundreds of miles away, were in my mind; had I done the right thing? It was about earning a living but was this really what I wanted to do with my life? My dreams of being a writer were going nowhere fast, as I realised that walking the landings inside The Scrubs was more poetic justice than poetry. My Great Aunt Norah had always said I would end up behind bars.

I must have eventually drifted off to sleep, for soon, my clock-work alarm was ringing and it was time to start a new career. It was just 7am, quite early, as I was not due at the jail till 9am. I quickly dressed in my brand new Prison Officer's uniform. Looking at myself in the wardrobe mirror, I didn't like the way the hat sat on my head, as it made me look like a car park attendant. I wore a casual jacket over the top of my uniform, tucked my hat under my arm, then set off, walking down Western Avenue onto Du Cane Road and, there before me, juxtaposed against the brilliant sunshine of a glorious May morning, I saw the huge dark oak and iron gates of HMP Wormwood Scrubs.

Inside the training unit, I met with all the new intake of staff and there was Paul. He looked like a real jailer in his uniform, six foot or so tall, with a big barrel chest and huge hands. We exchanged thoughts on our lodgings; he was sharing a room in a house on Old Oak Road, just around the corner from Carlisle Avenue, where I was staying. Paul seemed slightly ill at ease and I could sense there was something amiss; he just looked thirsty. We arranged to meet for a beer that night in the prison club situated directly outside the main gatehouse, something to look forward to.

Principal Officer M handed us individual timetables that would over the next two weeks and take us around the jail into all the different units. At this point, we were not issued with keys so, at each unit, we had to ring the bell at the locked gates and wait to be let in. A certain strict protocol had to be followed and, much as when I was at Strangeways, the unit's senior officer had to verify that we had been present and paid attention.

We were allocated a regular Prison Wing to attend each morning at 7am, to observe the counting and unlock procedure, which was followed by breakfast. I was placed on C Wing, which was the largest of the four wings and served as a local prison, taking all new adult male admissions from the local London courts. C Wing held approximately six hundred inmates, sharing around 300 cells on four landings connected by walkways and steep steel stairs. C2 landing was, in fact, the biggest single landing in Europe. It held around two hundred prisoners, mostly accommodated in shared cells, three men inside a twelve-foot by eight-foot cell.

The sanitation consisted of plastic pots and buckets that were emptied three times a day into one of the four recesses set into the walls along the landing. If Strangeways jail stank of piss and human excrement, then this place absolutely reeked of it. To control this huge landing, there were five staff; a senior officer located in a small cabin-like office and four discipline officers, each dealing with forty or so cells. At 11:30 hrs, on my first day in uniform as a Prison Officer, I was in C Wing and it seemed to me like organised chaos. Standing on C1 landing, watching as six hundred or so prisoners, one landing at a time, were unlocked, served their food on shiny stainless steel trays and locked up again within a matter of thirty minutes, was a sight to behold. The staff then counted the prisoners, reported their numbers to the landing senior officer, who subsequently shouted the landing total down to the duty Principal Officer: 'Two hundred and three on the Twos,' etc. Thus was the total number of inmates correctly accounted for.

I was scheduled to attend for an afternoon in the Hospital Annexe of the prison; this was located in a separate unit between A and B Wings, built on to the external wall. I rang the bell at the closed iron-barred gate; no response. Time passed, I rang again and I could hear it jingling somewhere inside the complex, but no one bothered to come. After about ten minutes or so, a Hospital Officer arrived; he was wearing a white tunic over uniform trousers, of middle height but powerfully built.

'You on induction?' he said in a deep Manchester accent and gave me an inquisitive stare.

That was something I was noticing about prison officers; many of them looked at you in a weirdly suspicious way. Inside the hospital, I was taken up a flight of stairs to an open ward, with around twenty beds spaced out along both sides. There were inmates in all manner of dress; some were in bed, others were wandering around with their prison clothing hanging loose, shirts open at the neck.

In the centre of the ward, at a long sturdy-looking table, sat a large bald-headed Hospital Officer, biro in hand, studying a half-completed crossword. I introduced myself and he motioned for me to take a seat next to him then, pushed the puzzle across. As luck would have it, he was doing the cryptic crossword of The Daily Telegraph, which was the one I sometimes managed to complete. Having answered a few of the clues, I passed it back and he seemed impressed.

'Cup of tea, John?' he said and, when I agreed that, yes, it would be nice, this affable Hospital Officer called over an inmate and said, 'Bring Mr Sutton a nice cup of tea.'

This was more like it, I thought, the Telegraph crossword, comfortable chair, a nice cup of tea and waiter service, too. I was instantly relaxed in what I perceived as a gentle and therapeutic atmosphere. The tea was truly excellent and served with some style by the inmate, who even brought me two ginger biscuits. How thoughtful was that? Taking the tea slowly, I enjoyed dipping in the ginger nuts and savouring the flavour of strong tea and sweetness.

'Have you met Graham?' the Hospital Officer asked me and, of course, I had not an idea to whom he was referring, so replied that, no, I was afraid I had not.

'The orderly who made your tea, Graham Young; you know, he poisoned his workmates, put parquet in the tea, murdered three of them.' He smiled.

For a moment, a horrible sickening feeling came over me. Looking up, I could see Graham Young close to my side, a strange twisted grin on his face.

'More tea, Mr Sutton?' he asked.

Within the hospital at The Scrubs, there was an experimental psychological unit that was straight out of the film, 'A Clockwork Orange'. It consisted of what looked like a dentist's chair, with a device that fitted onto the occupant's head, to measure their brainwaves, as before them, on a form of television screen, images were displayed. The Principal Hospital Officer operating this thing offered to give me a test run. He looked like a typical nutty professor, hair sticking up, wild eyes and long thin fingers that he wrapped around my wrist.

I was more than a little dubious but he assured me it was perfectly safe, though if these guys in this place thought having a convicted poisoner making their tea was safe, then maybe… well, I agreed to give it a go. The electrodes were attached to my head, mainly my forehead, and I was directed to watch the screen in front of me. The most revolting images began to appear but only briefly so I was, in effect, being bombarded with what I consciously thought were disgusting scenes of utter depravity, people being beaten, naked men and women being tortured; it seemed utterly horrible. The whole thing, though, lasted just a few minutes. When it was completed, the mad professor removed all the electrodes and gave me an unnerving stare.

'You could be a psychopath,' he whispered, getting a little too close for comfort. 'You like men, too.'

He gripped my wrist tightly, staring deeply into my eyes. I was out of there as soon as I could, believe me. It was later explained to me that the unit was experimenting with long-term sex offenders, who had committed the most horrendous crimes. The individuals were assessed by use of this device and then subjected to a con-trolled programme of psychotropic drugs, in an attempt to 'cure' them. Following a course of said drugs, they were then retested and their brainwaves measured, to see if the medication had, in fact, altered their response to the horrible images. So, it was really similar to the storyline of Stanley Kubrick's futuristic movie, 'A Clockwork Orange'. I was glad to get out of that disconcertingly strange place in one piece.

That night, I met with Paul, my boozing buddy, in the prison club just outside the main gatehouse and we shared our experi-ences of what had so far transpired. He had been allocated to B Wing, which was the Borstal Allocation Unit, and he said it had its own unique problems, mainly that the inmates were little more than boys, who had virtually no self-discipline. Almost everything required to get them through the day had to be shouted at the Borstal Trainees as a direct order. It seemed there was a lot of noise in B Wing, as staff dealt with highly immature youths, accustomed to getting all their own way, which was something they certainly would not get in The Scrubs.

The Prison Officers' Club reminded me a great deal of an NCO's bar in the Army; officers in uniform mingled with those in civilian dress and the beer was good enough at a reasonable price.

Over quite a few pints, I got the chance to talk to Paul about much more than jails. He was a big heavy man, rather Falstaffian in both appearance and demeanour, with an immense capacity for booze. Paul was, despite his tendency to imbibe more than was good for him, a man of learning, with a vast knowledge of literature and the arts. He was, he advised, a great lover of the works of Shakespeare and he wondered if I would like to see a production of 'Richard III', being staged at a new theatre, not too far from Wormwood Scrubs. Never having had the inclination or really the opportunity to see a Shakespearian play in a profes- sional theatre, I agreed, especially as the role of Richard III was being played by the brilliant Alan Badel, who had featured in one of my favourite films with Richard Harris; 'This Sporting Life'.

More beer followed and Paul's ability to continue conversing about literature, or anything else for that matter, began to fail. He could still drink, though, but not speak, which proved a serious impediment when he decided to telephone his wife, back home in Liverpool. We were standing by the entrance to the club where the pay-phone was on the wall and he had somehow managed to dial the correct number, which I assume was duly answered by his dearly beloved. I could see Paul was trying to speak; he smiled and opened his mouth, but no words came out. After a few moments, he passed me the handset.

'Hello,' I said, 'Paul is here.'

The voice at the other end belonged to an obviously Liverpudlian lady. 'Who are you?' she asked and I did my best to explain that Paul and I were colleagues at The Scrubs and he was calling to say he loved her, but…

'But he's pissed again, isn't he?'

With that, the phone went dead and she was gone.

'Says she loves you, Paul,' I lied.

He smiled a contented peaceful smile, before slowly slipping to the ground, where he instantly fell asleep and started snoring.

CHAPTER 7

A HAUNTING EXPERIENCE

At the end of the induction period, I was issued with a Home Office Warrant Card and allocated a set of keys that opened the security gates and the cells. I was now officially a Prison Officer or 'Screw', as jailers are traditionally known. My permanent posting was to C Wing, where the Principal Officer scheduled me as part of the team on C2 landing. This was about as tough a posting as existed within the Prison Service; on this landing, not only were there over two hundred inmates, but also a number of Category A prisoners, on special watch. These inmates had to be unlocked separately and each had a movement booklet that required completion and signing, whenever the Cat A was moved from place to place, so it went with the escorting officer.

The senior officer in charge of C2 was Scottish, big, broad-shouldered and a former S.A.S. NCO in the Army, similar to my own background, except this character had served with the Special Air Services. The landing was really busy, as one may imagine, with over two hundred prisoners, all requiring attention. Most of the prisoners accepted that they were there by their own hand and had to get on with it; they called the officers Guv or Guvn'r. I did notice, however, that there was a slight degree of racial tension, as approximately thirty percent of the prison population in Wormwood Scrubs was from ethnic minority groups.

At the time, the predominant minority ethnic group were the second-generation West Indians, with families from the Caribbean Basin, or Jamaica, ex-colonial territories. There was prejudice and it was not, as far as I could see, initiated by the staff. The insults we received while going about our daily duties were mainly incomprehensible, as the language in which they were delivered was not English, but a form of Rastafarian patois. I was frequently referred to as 'Bumbaclot' or 'Rasclot', terms that actually meant nothing to me but they seemed to amuse the dreadlock-wearing West Indian inmates, who muttered these as I helped them into their cells and gently locked the door.

I had now been in Wormwood Scrubs for what, to me, seemed a reasonable amount of time and went to see the chairman of the branch of the Prison Officer's Association. I needed to ask how I went about applying for accommodation, to bring my wife, Mary, to London. She was still living back in our rented flat at Leigh in Lancashire and I had been travelling home every other weekend. I had asked a few more senior staff about housing and they all said the best thing was to go see the POA, as the Chairman sat on what was termed The Housing Committee.

It seemed that the Chairman was, in fact, a Principal Officer, whose duties included running the Staff Rota for HMP Wormwood Scrubs. I went to see this PO, Mr B, and asked if he could arrange for me to speak to him regarding the allocation of married families accommodation. He gave me a cursory glance and said something about me only having just arrived, so there would be no point in me even applying. This just did not seem reasonable to me, as I had understood that The Home Office provided housing for staff and their families on posting and I had been posted to London from Manchester. That, PO Mr B explained, was not actually the case; HMP Wormwood Scrubs was my first posting, not Strangeways, Manchester, so I was a new member of staff and would have to wait my turn. When I asked how long I should expect to have to wait, he smiled and said a minimum of six months would be usual before submitting an application to the housing committee. It was now the middle of July and that would mean I could not even apply until the middle of November. That evening, I telephoned Mary and told her what I had discovered. She was quite calm about it and suggested I have a look at finding some private rental, a small flat maybe, like we had in Leigh. I set off immediately to make enquiries and my landlady at Carlisle Avenue suggested I visit the local estate agent, helping me to find their telephone number in the Yellow Pages directory.

Prison Officers working as Discipline grades in the jails are required, as part of their duties, to undertake night shifts. These operate on a rota and run for seven consecutive nights, Friday to Friday, 9pm to 7am. Inside the walls at 8:45pm on the Friday of my first tour of duty on nights, I reported to the duty Principal Officer and was allocated D Wing. This was the long-term wing of the prison, where many of the inmates were serving life sentences or terms in excess of ten years or so. I had been in and through D Wing a number of times during my day shifts, but never before at night.

What I was instructed to do was patrol the landings and, at least twice an hour on the half hour, turn a key in a metal box, located at the top far end of the fourth landing and at the bottom opposite end of the first landing. By turning the key, I registered a signal in the main office that was recorded on a scroll, to show that I had continuously carried out my duties and patrolled the landings, as required. Everything in D Wing was locked up and, being on nights, I had no keys. There was a telephone if I needed to call for assistance, but there was no way I could let anyone in or out and all the inmates were secured behind their cell doors.

There is something extremely spooky about the inside of a prison after midnight in the witching hours, especially so when you are on your own. I found myself listening to the silence and was completely convinced that I heard footsteps ascending the metal stairs, as I walked along the dark shadowed landing of D4. Outside, the silver moonlight shone brightly, filtering in through the high windows set into the end wall of D Wing. It was from within this prison unit, through that very window, that the notorious spy, George Blake, had escaped, in October of 1966. Behind the doors of these cells surrounding me now, were some of the most dangerous prisoners in the UK. The Great Train Robbers were in there, Gordon Goody and Jim Hussey; there were members of the IRA and numerous murderers serving life sentences.

There was an eerie stillness about the place; the odd scratching sound indicated something was moving, a loathsome rat perhaps, clawing at the sewer pipes. A bell rang! Each cell had an alarm bell for the inmate occupant to press and summon a member of staff, in the case of emergency. The location of the alarm call registered on a board, indicating which landing and cell had summoned assistance. I checked and it was the very end cell of D4 landing. It took me a few moments to get there and I tapped on the cell door. It was extremely cold, preternaturally cold, distinctly chilly, and a slight shudder ran through me. I began asking the inmate, quietly and calmly, what the problem was. I peered through the Judas spy hole in the door and saw, in the dim light, the prisoner standing, staring at me a look of terror in his eyes.

'There's a woman in me cell, Guv! A woman in a long grey dress, sitting on me bed… Get me out, Guv! GUV!'

The man was obviously deluded, as this was an all-male prison and there simply were no women at all within the walls of Wormwood Scrubs, on this dark moonlit night. I spoke gently to the poor troubled soul and explained that he was dreaming; this was nothing more than a nightmare and he should rest, all would be well. I told him my name was John and that he was absolutely safe, nothing could harm him, as I was there. It took me at least twenty minutes or so to calm this man down, but slowly, he accepted that he had imagined the vision of the woman and agreed to go back to bed and get some sleep.

The rest of that first night passed completely without incident and, at 6am, as the sunlight streamed in through the windows, I felt a strange sense of achievement. I had successfully undertaken my first night shift without a problem, or so I thought. The duty Senior Officer came in to collect the scroll from the main office that had recorded all my turnings of the key, twice an hour on the hour and at half past, except I hadn't. He did not look best pleased when he examined the scroll and called me over, asking me to explain why, at 01:00 hrs, I had failed to turn the key on the D1 terminal. That was when I was dealing with the alarm bell at the end cell of D4, I explained, and showed my entry in the incident book.

'What did he want?' the Senior Officer asked and I just told him how the man had imagined he had seen a woman dressed in grey, sitting on his bed, and how I had explained that he was dreaming, as this was an all-male prison and there were no women here.

'There used to be women here,' the Senior Officer replied. 'This wing, in the 1920s, served as the women's prison and there was a suicide. A female inmate jumped to her death from D4 Landing, right at that very end. Many people, staff included, have seen her ghost. She is always dressed in grey.'

A little tingle of fear danced down my spine, as I looked up to the far end of D4 landing and, for a brief moment, I recalled the phantom footsteps and that mysterious unearthly chill that had surrounded the prisoner's cell.

On Saturday afternoons, the inmates of C Wing were given the opportunity to attend a screening of a film, in a converted building some hundred or so yards from the exterior exercise yard, at the side of the cell block. This particular afternoon, I was called into the Wing PO's office and he assigned me the duty of taking a Category A prisoner under close guard, to watch the movie 'Vault of Horror', which was supposed to be a gruesome X-rated shocker.

Handcuffed to me was a Cat A inmate, recently convicted and awaiting sentence for murdering a number of prostitutes in central London and drinking their blood. The tabloid press had sensationalised his crimes and named him 'The Soho Vampire'. He looked the part; emaciated, tall, long grey straggly hair, sallow features, staring with cold dark psychopathic eyes and prominent teeth. In fact, he was practically a double of the movie vampire, Nosferatu. He said nothing as we walked across to the makeshift cinema, just stared blankly ahead and followed my instructions. I directed him to sit next to me at the rear of the unit, close to the exit.

The place was packed front to back with prisoners, who were seated quietly, waiting for the film to start. When it did, my hand-cuffed Cat A began a sort of deep guttural growling and started to get restless. No wonder, as the first part of this horror movie depicted the murder of a beautiful young woman, who mysteri-ously came back to life as a vampire. Her killer was subsequently captured by hordes of the undead, who then proceeded to hang him upside down and insert a form of tap into his jugular vein, from which they took turns to drink his blood.

When my prisoner, 'The Soho Vampire', saw this, he started howling like a banshee, jumped up and tried to grab me by the throat, slavering and gnashing his teeth. Instinctively, I punched him in the face with my clenched fist, which caused his nose to spurt blood, yet still he struggled. Around us, all hell broke loose, as inmates began running away, no doubt fearful that they would become a victim of this madman. I obviously could not escape, as he was handcuffed to me, so I fought him off; another right hook with my fist knocked him to the floor, where I attempted to subdue the man. Other staff ran to my aid and, between us, we dragged this screaming, struggling inmate out of the place, across the exercise yard and into C Wing, where we locked him in one of the empty segregated cells on C1.

I was seriously happy to get those cuffs off; imagine taking 'The Soho Vampire' to watch a movie about vampires! Whose mad idea was that, I wondered? Then I recalled it was the Wing PO, who had personally given me that detail and I knew from other sources that he was with The Brotherhood; he was a Freemason. Later that afternoon, 'The Soho Vampire' was removed from C Wing and relocated to a padded cell inside the prison hospital. I learned, many weeks later, that he had been certified under The Mental Health Act and transferred to a secure psychiatric hospital for the criminally insane.

Working as a Discipline Officer on the landings of C Wing in HMP Wormwood Scrubs was mainly a series of mundane tasks, enabling the inmates to be contained, fed, accommodated and processed by the system. The basic duties were, in themselves, rather boring; supervising bathing, counting prisoners, organising library visits, counting prisoners, feeding inmates, counting prisoners, and so on. It was the characters within the jail itself that made the job interesting and there were many of those.

One such was a powerfully built Irishman, called John C. He was a prison officer who had been posted to The Scrubs, following a series of unfortunate incidents at HMP Brixton, where he had been serving. John C was, without doubt, what you would term a dangerous man to know and I knew him. For some unknown reason, he and I got on really well and I found him to be a highly amusing and entertaining individual to work with. But it was not always so. The first time I encountered John C, he gave me great cause for concern. It was during a late evening shift that I was scheduled to work alongside John C on the YP or Young Offenders unit, located in B Wing.

This was a sectioned-off unit of two landings, containing approximately one hundred young prisoners; that is, inmates aged between eighteen and twenty-one years of age. The shift stated at 17:30 hrs and ended at 21:00 hrs; in between that time, John C and I had to open up the inmates, slop them out, that is, allow them to empty their pots and buckets, get fresh water and use the toilets, then lock them in. Following this, we had to take round hot sweet tea and a bun to each inmate, again lock them in and this was followed by counting them and calling in the total to the central control office. Straightforward and rather mundane duty, you may well think, and so it should have been, but I was working with John C.

All was going smoothly; it was around 19:45 hrs and we had completed the slopping out. John C took delivery of the tea and buns for the YP unit. He counted the exact number of buns on three metal trays and three stainless steel buckets of hot sweet tea. There were two inmate orderlies, who carried the tea and buns. I went first, opening the cells, with the orderlies handing out one bun per prisoner and scooping up the tea in a mug, then pouring it into the inmates' mugs. The whole process took around ten minutes, till we arrived at the last cell and there was one bun short.

Now, John C had counted all the buns, so he knew exactly how many there were; one bun each for all the inmates of the YP unit. John C was not amused by this, I could see that.

'Go lock yourself in the office,' he said to me.

There being a glint of madness in his eyes, I decided it was wise to do exactly that. So, I went into the glass-fronted office unit, closed and secured the door behind me, and took a seat behind the desk, from which I had a clear view of the YP landings. What I saw next astounded me; I could hardly believe it. John C opened the first cell, containing three young prisoners, all strapping fit youths.

He shouted, 'Who stole the bun?'

No reply, so he proceeded to belt all three of the inmates, slapping and punching them so hard, they fell to the ground, screaming for mercy. He then slammed the cell door shut, walked to the next cell and repeated the process once again.

'Who stole the bun?'

No reply, crash bang wallop, screaming and crying inmates on the floor. The orderlies were hiding in their cells. I watched, transfixed with terror, as I feared he would seriously injure one of these young prisoners and they were not children; these were big hulking twenty-year-old thugs who, months before, had been mugging and robbing people on the streets of London. Now they were getting ten shades of shit beaten out of them, by one huge and powerful Irishman. I honestly did not know what to do, so I called the duty Principal Officer and asked for advice, as I was seriously worried that this maniac may decide I had stolen his precious bun and set about me.

The PO answered the phone and, when I told him what was

happening, he just laughed. 'First time working with John C?' he said. 'You'll get used to it.'

John C went on to batter ten bells out of every single prisoner on the YP unit, till he came to the last cell, the orderlies' cell. There he found the answer he had supposedly been looking for; there was the missing bun. The orderly handing them out had placed his own bun in his cell before starting out to deliver the rest. John C just shrugged his shoulders, locked them in and motioned for me to come out of the office.

'You can count them now,' he said.

CHAPTER 8

HARD-BOILED INMATES

There were days when I was scheduled to work in various units other than C Wing and, on one such occasion, I was allocated a shift in the high-security segregation unit, located at the far end of A Wing. This unit had a specially selected and trained staff, who dealt with the most difficult and dangerous prisoners in the system. Some of the inmates within the high-security unit were not even identified by name and the cell cards outside their individual cells displayed only their security rating i.e. Cat A E-List. Some inmates, I learned, were considered to be so dangerous, they were only unlocked when there was a minimum of three strong staff and at least one dog handler, with a huge German Shepherd dog present.

On this day, I was to be one of the strong staff detailed to be there whenever a certain prisoner without a name was unlocked. The shift started at 07:00 hrs and I was required to be in that unit, ready for duty at that time, which meant getting there early, as I did not have a key to access the high-security area and had to ring the bell.

The high-security unit at Wormwood Scrubs consisted of two landings of cells, contained within a heavy-duty razor wire fence that is inside the sixteen-foot-high walls of the jail. There were approximately twenty single occupancy cells within this unit and they held many of the most notorious prisoners in the system. At the time, the inmates included ex-police officers imprisoned for corruption, numerous IRA terrorists, one notorious child killer, various violent inmates serving terms of segregation for assaulting staff or other inmates and the prisoner with no name.

I was told to stand by the nameless inmate's cell door and observe the procedure. This started with a one cell at a time slop out and bang up, with two muscular-looking officers standing by each inmate as they went to and from the recess. The last to be unlocked was the unnamed prisoner and, for this, a dog handler had to be brought into the unit. I was really interested to see what was so special about the man behind this door, that he had to be so securely guarded. The two muscle-bound jailers came to my side, the dog handler was close by and then they unlocked him.

The man that came out was about five foot six inches tall, but broad with a big barrel chest, close-cropped dark hair and virtually no neck. His arms were long and I noticed he had wide short hands that he kept clenching into fists as he moved slowly along the landing in bare feet. Once he was inside the recess, I was prodded by the biggest of the two jailers, then pushed forward so I had to enter the urinal with the mysterious inmate, standing directly next to him as he deliberately pissed all over my boots. In a language I knew to be French, he whispered, 'Emmerder, Monsieur,' (it roughly translates as Piss Off Mister). I could hear a somewhat sinister chuckle behind me as this seemed to amuse the two jailers, who had obviously witnessed the routine before, but I could do nothing about it.

Once the unnamed inmate was securely locked behind his door again, there followed what I can only describe as a truly bizarre ritual. The breakfast for the occupants of the high-security unit consisted of cornflakes or porridge with slices of bread, a spoonful of jam and a hard-boiled egg, with a cup of tea. That may seem like nothing unusual but, and this is where it became really weird, all the hard-boiled eggs had writing on them in bold black marker pen ink. One said, 'Bent Copper', another said, 'Child Killer'. The staff had written the name of the crimes committed by the inmates of the unit on the eggs. When they came to collect their breakfast, they had to select the egg that matched their crime.

I watched as, one by one, each was unlocked and, at the

hot-plate where breakfast was served, they did indeed take the egg that carried the name of their offence. The ex-CID Metropolitan Police Chief Superintendent Moody picked up his 'Bent Copper' hard-boiled egg, Ian Brady, the Moors Murderer, a notorious violator of little children, selected his 'Child Killer' egg, and so on. The prisoner with no name was the exception; his breakfast was placed in his cell and, as far as I could see, his egg was unmarked. I later asked one of the staff what happened if they took the wrong egg and he just laughed. I gathered that inmates in that unit only made such a mistake once.

During my day in the high-security unit, I was detailed to work the late lunch shift and patrol the landings, along with a senior member of staff, who remained in the unit's office. It would be around 12:45 hrs when I was called in to that office, where the senior officer told me an important visitor was coming to visit the notorious child killer. I was cautioned that, at no time, was I to go near the open cell of said inmate during this visit, as this visitor had the express authority of the Prison Governor to conduct his visit to the prisoner in private in his cell.

Being curious, I asked who on earth this could be, as it seemed to me to be against all security protocol, since the life-sentence prisoner in question was on the Category A list. There followed a strange silence, as the senior officer gave me one of those jailer stares I was quickly becoming accustomed to.

'He's from The Government and you may recognise him when you see him, but you must say nothing and keep out of his way. Do You Understand?'

Well, of course I did understand when I saw the expensively-dressed, rather large gentleman walk into the unit, with his supercilious aristocratic nose stuck up in the air, completely ignoring me. He was really expensively attired, bespoke tailoring Turnbull and Asser of Jermyn Street London-style, pin-striped suit, all absolutely immaculate. The senior officer personally, rather obsequiously I thought, shook his hand and I saw the 'gentleman' smile, as if he had received a secret coded message.

The SO escorted him to the cell of Ian Brady, the notorious child killer, the Moors Murderer, opened it up and let the gentleman in, shooting the bolt so the door could not lock and then drawing it to behind him.

Now, this seriously intrigued me. Why, I wondered, would this eminent personage from Westminster want to visit such an odious creature as that murderer of young children? I had to stay away, of course; I could not get too close, but I listened carefully and there were little odd noises coming from that cell. My senses told me this was fundamentally wrong, so I maintained a discreet distance and kept my eyes open. It was some twenty or so minutes later that the large gentleman came out of the cell and headed, rather hastily it seemed to me, for the exit.

I positioned myself close by the heavy metal door leading in and out of the security unit, so I could get a good look at this individual, and his appearance had changed. No longer was he so pristine in presentation, no more did he exude absolute authority; he now appeared flushed, his face slightly sweaty and red, his previously immaculate attire decidedly dishevelled. His shirt collar was twisted into disarray and his tie was somewhat awry. Again, he totally avoided looking at me, as if I were something utterly beneath his contempt, but he shook the senior officer's hand again in a strange exaggerated manner and made a hasty exit through the heavy steel door when he opened it.

I tried to engage the senior officer in conversation concerning what had just transpired but, when I told him that, yes, I had recognised the visitor, he just gave me another jailer's glare and said, 'Visitor? I saw no one at all and neither did you. Do You Understand?'

I was certainly beginning to. It struck me that this was how The Brotherhood maintained their invisibility; no one dared to mention their presence.

Another aspect of my duties at The Scrubs was Home Office productions to court; that is, inmates held in the jail, who were required to appear at Magistrates or Crown Court had to be transported there under escort. There were usually two officers to one prisoner being produced at court; the junior jailer was normally handcuffed to the inmate, while the more senior officer managed all the paperwork.

It was late July, a scorching summer's day, when I found myself once again working with the wild Irishman Prison Officer, John C. Since I had endured that evening on the YP Unit, when he had beaten the living daylights out of over one hundred young offenders, I had got to know the man. We had shared a few pints of Guinness in the prison club and I had managed to get a little of his story from him. John C was notorious, not only at The Scrubs, where most staff refused to work with him as he was considered dangerous, but also at HMP Brixton, where he had worked previously. John C told me how he had managed to find himself posted to The Scrubs and it was quite an amazing series of events, the way he told it.

John C had been a Discipline Officer at Brixton, which was a remand prison, holding inmates awaiting trial in the Central London Criminal Courts, including The Old Bailey. Onto his landing in Brixton came two infamous villains, noted for being violent men; they were Ronnie and Reggie Kray, known as The Kray Twins. John C explained that, before these two thugs arrived on his landing, he had maintained good order and discipline, with a minimum of trouble. He had slapped one or two of the so-called tough guys and so, when John C said get behind your door, the prisoners did exactly that. It made good sense to me and I liked his direct style, no messing; either do what John C says or stand by for action.

Then, along came the Kray Twins, who believed they could continue on the inside what they had started on the streets of London; that is, ruling with terror tactics. Unfortunately for Ronnie and Reggie, they found themselves facing six foot two inches and seventeen stone of one uncompromising Irishman called John C. The way he told it, there was no actual physical force used; John C said he just walked into the Kray Twins' cell, bumped the pair of them against the wall and advised that there was only one hard man in HMP Brixton and it wasn't either of them. One wrong move and John C promised them the best good hiding they had ever had in their lives.

From that moment on, whenever Ronnie or Reggie clapped eyes on John C, they would lock themselves up. But they had friends and word got round that John C was going to meet a brutal end. It seemed that The Governor of HMP Brixton was warned about this and took John C off the prison landings and put him in charge of opening and closing the huge inner iron gates of HMP Brixton, which duty John C took seriously.

In the early 1970s, while John C was working the iron gates, a group of villains attempted to break out of HMP Brixton by ramming those gates in the dustbin wagon they had commandeered. John C was on the gates that day and, when the huge bin wagon smashed into them, he went into action. John C explained he had grabbed a large lump of wood from the contents of the bin wagon, and jumped up and into the cabin of the vehicle, where he began beating the inmates into unconsciousness with this weapon.

In John's mind, he was a hero; he had saved the gates from further damage and prevented a break-out from the prison. In the eyes of The Governor, John C was a dangerous man, who had hospitalised three prisoners, injuring them to such an extent that they all needed prolonged medical treatment. John C seemed quite philosophical about the matter; The Governor had a different view and so, following a disciplinary hearing, he was transferred from HMP Brixton to HMP Wormwood Scrubs.

We were taking a prisoner from The Scrubs on production to Bow Street Magistrates Court, in Central London. I was cuffed to the inmate and John C took all the papers, to hand to the court officers. The transport through London was by HMP Secure Van, with bars at the rear window and generally strengthened. Once at Bow Street, we reported in to the duty Police Sergeant running the cells and having examined the production order, he asked John C to remove the handcuffs and located our prisoner inside a convenient cell. We took a seat and made ourselves at home, as best we could.

Bow Street court in 1975 was located in its original building and, in the cellars below, which is where we were now, there were various cells and a large iron cage, in which those arrested the previous day were held. That cage consisted of thick iron bars set into the floor and ceiling, with a stone wall behind. The current crop of prisoners in there included many women, dressed in all manner of outlandish outfits. We were sitting just a few yards away from this open cage, so I casually asked one young lady how on earth she had managed to find herself in such a place.

'Lifted me in the Dilly dear. My turn, I reckon.'

Which, to me, was an incomprehensible response but John C explained that these were street-walkers, common prostitutes, who had been arrested during the night and were awaiting an appearance before the Magistrates Court. The Dilly was, of course, Piccadilly, a road in London adjoining Regent Street.

There was a separate cage unit next to the one holding the ladies of the night. This cage held men; well, just two men, to be exact, and one of them was a large and loud black Rastafarian dreadlocked individual, who was continuously shouting abuse at the Police Sergeant.

'Hey, ya Rass Clot man, ya open me up, I need da toilet, man!'

On and on and on he shouted, until the policeman decided to let him out. The Sergeant was not a particularly big man, slightly taller than average but next to the hulking great Rasta man, he appeared quite small. I watched with little real interest as the policeman led this large prisoner to the toilets; it seemed perfectly routine to me, until I heard the almightiest scream. John C and I jumped up and ran across the room to the toilet area, where we saw that the massive prisoner had grabbed the Sergeant by the neck and was throttling him.

I heard John C whistle and then he shouted, 'Head to the left, Captain.'

The next second, the huge black Rasta man was on the floor,

unconscious, his legs twitching as if he had been pole-axed. Well, in a way he had; John C had landed a straight right on his chin and switched the lights off. I attended to the policeman and made sure he was OK, there being no real damage, as he had just been shaken up by the attack, which was not exactly the case with the big Rastafarian man, who was still flat out and shaking from head to foot. I could see the colour drain from the Police Sergeant's face as he looked down at his would-be assailant.

It took almost ten minutes or so to bring the prisoner round and, even then, he seemed totally disorientated. The Sergeant was in serious panic mode and began demanding a statement from me, as to what I had seen. His obvious intention was to cover his own backside and drop John C in it for felling his attacker. I really did my best to recall what I had seen; it seemed, from where I was standing, that the prisoner had been attempting to strangle the policeman and, in the course of so doing, had slipped, fallen and bumped his head on the stone floor. That was exactly what John C had seen as well, so we quickly wrote out our statements, signed them and gave these to the Police Sergeant, whose life we had just saved. He could do exactly what he wanted with them. I had one or two ideas about the best place to file them.

It was the fifth of August 1975, our wedding anniversary, and my twenty-sixth birthday was on the sixth. I had booked Mary and myself in for two nights at The Holiday Inn to celebrate. However, disaster had befallen Mary as, just days before, she was in a club watching The Drifters live on stage, had gone to the washroom, where she had slipped on the wet floor and split-fractured a bone in her right leg. Now she was in plaster and could not walk, so my mother had agreed to help and come with her on the train to London Euston, where I would meet them off the four-fifteen from Manchester.

This was far more complicated than one might imagine as, some weeks before, I had sold my old Triumph Herald and bought a two-seater MGB open-top sports car. So, I had to borrow a colleague's saloon car, collect them, drive to the Holiday Inn, and return later in my MGB. I managed the first part without too much trouble and we all got checked in to our hotel rooms and off I went to change cars.

I was in my MGB, driving along the A406, otherwise known as the North Circular Road. There was, as usual, heavy traffic and I was in the outside lane, doing perhaps 50mph. As I came to a junction, the lights began to change; I could slam on the brakes and risk being rear-ended by the car directly behind me, or go through on amber. I made the wrong choice and, as I came to the middle of the junction, a car that had been waiting to turn did so right into my path and we collided. The front driver's side of my MGB disintegrated and my head bounced off the windscreen pillar, splitting the flesh wide open. The blood was spurting out from my forehead like a crimson fountain and I was totally disorientated, but not unconscious.

The ambulance came and I was soon in the Accident and Emergency unit, having around fifteen or so sutures applied to my wound. I must have had the sense to telephone Mary at the Holiday Inn, as I recall she quickly arrived at the hospital with my mother. We looked a right pair, Mary with her leg in plaster and me with a large bandage around my head, like some Eastern mystic. Eventually, we got a taxi and made our way back to The Holiday Inn, where I virtually collapsed.

The next morning, the sixth of August, my birthday and our wedding anniversary, I was on duty at The Scrubs and had to be there at 7am so, at 5:30am, Mary arranged a taxi and I set off back to my lodgings, some nine miles away. I felt unwell; the wound to my head was just a dull ache but my body was shaking with a form of delayed shock. At 6am, I was in my room at Carlisle Avenue, getting changed into uniform and doing my best to conceal the bandage with my prison officer's hat.

Somehow, I made it into the jail and began my shift on C Wing. I had applied for a day's leave but it was the summertime and the long service staff with children had booked all the available places. So I was doomed to work on our special day; at least, that was the plan, until I started to shake uncontrollably. I had just completed supervising the serving of breakfast on C Wing, when the duty Principal Officer saw me trembling and staggering along the landing. I explained about the car crash, showed him the bandaged wound and he immediately advised I report in sick and seek medical assistance.

I had not as yet registered with a Doctor so, unless I went back to the hospital, I was on my own. Having reported in sick at The Scrubs, I slowly made my way down Du Cane Road, back to my lodgings and went to bed. The shaking was uncontrollable; all my limbs trembled and I kept seeing visions of my MGB, smashed to pieces. The landlady had asked me if I was going to be OK and seemed concerned; I assured her I was, but I just needed to rest. It was late afternoon when I awoke, still shaking slightly but fit to travel. At around 5pm, I arrived by taxi back at The Holliday Inn in Wimbledon to meet with Mary and my mother.

I took the lift up to the floor and went quietly along to our room, knocked on the door and was expecting Mary to answer; no reply. I knocked again, but no one came to the door and I had no key. I went back down to reception and asked if they could telephone the room and wake Mary up, as I felt sure she must have been in there, deeply asleep. She wasn't. The receptionist explained there had been an accident and that our room had been moved; we were now on a different floor in a different room. By this time, I was beginning to think we were cursed.

When I finally found Mary in the new room, she explained what had happened. After a tiring long day of being dragged round London with her leg in plaster, sightseeing with my mother, she had returned to our room and fallen asleep only to be woken minutes later by a torrent of water pouring in from the ceiling, drenching her, the bed and everything around it. All Mary's clothes were soaked, the suitcase was dripping wet and so were its contents, my shirt and trousers, etc. When she contacted reception, they checked and found that the occupant of the room directly above had fallen asleep in the bath with the taps running, so it had overflowed, flooding the floor, then drained through the ceiling down directly on to Mary, fast asleep below.

'Happy Anniversary, dear,' I said, presenting her with the red roses I had somehow remembered to buy. 'I think these need water.'

The problems surrounding Mary's visit to London were, I am now quite certain, a sign to me that I was not yet ready to understand. My psychic ability was in an early stage and, though able to observe paranormal phenomena, I was as yet unable to decipher the meaning. Often, when something is not meant to be, or will prove extremely unfortunate, the universe has a way of letting you know. Those with developed psychic powers can see and decode the messages that Carl Jung the psychologist termed 'Synchronicity'. All the signs around Mary and me in London were terrible. Had I, at that time, got my psychic gift to a higher stage of development, I would doubtless have recognised the warning that the universe was giving me. Of course, I did not and so ignored the alarm bells that were ringing and continued on what, from that point on, proved to be a pathway to perdition.

CHAPTER 9

POLTERGEIST ATTACK

It was the middle of August and I had been in my new posting as a Prison Officer at HMP Wormwood Scrubs since May, so three months. It seemed to me it was time to apply for a prison quarter and bring Mary to London, as living in lodgings and travelling home every other weekend was causing me problems. My boozing buddy Paul and I were doing far too much drinking and I simply had to stop that, as it was making me ill. There had to be something more to life than going to the pub every night, so I made some enquiries and found that, in Ealing, some few miles north of The Scrubs, there was a college offering part-time courses, accredited by London University. I decided to apply to study sociology at diploma level, which would give me credits for a subsequent degree. The applications for places were required in August for start in early September, so I went along and submitted my completed documents. The Home Office had an education department and, if accepted on the Sociology Diploma course, I could apply to them for a grant to cover the costs involved. To my great delight, I was accepted by Ealing College and sent a reading list. The course was taught once a week, from 6pm to 9pm on Thursday nights.

Every five weeks, the housing committee at The Scrubs posted up a list of properties available for staff and applications from entitled officers were invited. I recalled what the chairman of the committee had told me, that there was no point in applying till I had at least six months service in, but I ignored that and completed the form, which I duly submitted. There were just three properties available and at least twenty or so officers on the waiting list, but I thought I had to try, as Mary was over two hundred miles away and, as far as I was concerned, this was totally not right, since my contract said I would be offered accommodation.

I called Mary up and gave her the news about my London University Sociology course; she was really pleased that I would be writing again, as I had neglected that for too long. When I explained about the application to the housing committee, she was less enthusiastic and thought there was absolutely no chance. But somehow, I knew this was not a foregone conclusion. Since I had that awful car crash, badly scarring my head and terribly traumatising me, I had started to experience what I termed visions. I just knew certain things were going to happen; it was as if I had awakened a sixth sense.

I was patrolling C2 landing early one afternoon, when I saw along the walkway, some distance in front of me, a mysterious dark shadowy shape appear and almost instantly disappear, as if it had gone through a closed cell door. Split seconds later, I heard the most horrendous screaming coming from inside the cell into which I seen the shadow vanish. There followed a series of seriously loud banging sounds, as if some mad giant was slamming a metal locker against the cell walls. The screams were getting louder and whoever was inside began thumping frantically on the door.

Within seconds, I was at the cell in question and, it being early afternoon with staff on duty, I had no reason not to unlock the door and see what this tremendous racket was all about. When I pulled open the door, two inmates almost jumped out on me and grabbed the steel railings at the side of the landing; they appeared terrified. I looked inside and saw on the floor a prisoner, curled up in the foetal position with his hands over his head. The cell was deadly cold, there was rubbish everywhere and, to my utter amazement, the beds, all three of them, appeared to be floating in mid-air.

'Get him out, Guv!' screamed one of the prisoners behind me. 'Get him out!'

In an instant, I reached down and grabbed the man on the floor by the back of his shirt collar and physically heaved him out of the cell onto the walkway, where he lay, sobbing and staring, wild-eyed, like a man possessed.

By this time, other staff had joined me and I was able to take a moment to ask the former inmates of that cell just exactly what this was all about. It seemed they were bored being banged up all the time and had decided to create a homemade Ouija Board. They had then used this, asking the usual question, 'Is there anybody there?' Unfortunately for them, there was. When the entity answered their call, it did so with dynamic and destructive effect.

Suddenly, a powerful freezing wind had blown into the cell, followed almost instantly by a mighty dark shapeless shadowy something that threw their beds into the air and began battering them against the cell walls. The inmate still on the floor had been, they said, thrown up to the ceiling and then suspended in mid-air. I had seen the levitating beds myself, so there was no doubt in my mind that these three amateur occultists had opened the invisible door between this world and the next, allowing what I believed to be a poltergeist in and that was what had wrecked their cell and scared them witless.

Someone called the duty Hospital Officer and he tended to the still collapsed inmate. I locked the cell up and relocated the other two prisoners, while their demented cell mate was carried away to the padded cells on a stretcher. When I submitted my written report on this incident to the Wing Principal Officer, he screwed it up and threw it at me.

'Utter bollocks, Mr Sutton!' he shouted and pointed at the door, through which I had just entered. 'Close it behind you.'

D Wing, the long-term prisoners' unit, was short of staff one week and I was seconded there, to work as a Discipline Officer on the landings. On my first day, the Principal Officer in charge called me into his office and gave me some advice, to the effect that the inmates on this wing were allowed a great deal more privileges than those on C Wing, where I normally worked. I was told to watch the way the regular D Wing staff went about their duties and basically not make any waves.

The reasoning behind this much more relaxed regime was that the prisoners within the wing were serving long sentences. Though still considered to be highly dangerous, they were given more leeway within the confines of the unit as, that way, they behaved themselves. That was the theory and, as a general rule, it worked. I sensed that the atmosphere within D Wing was less tense and the inmates appeared at ease with the staff. There were certainly no jailers shouting direct orders and mealtimes were completely casual, rather civilised affairs, with inmates sharing cells to dine together.

On the surface, D Wing looked like a wonderfully easy place to be a Prison Officer, but I could see there was something seriously dark beneath that thin veneer of tranquillity. Just looking at some of the prisoners sent a shiver down my spine, as they faked their obsequious smiles, sniggering secretly behind their long-practised masks. D Wing was not what it appeared to be and I was in no way about to be lulled into any false sense of security by inmates who were masters of manipulation and deception.

I was given the task of changing the inmates' laundry. This involved taking all the dirty sheets, shirts, pillowcases, vests, socks, underclothing, etc, to the central laundry unit and exchanging these on a one-for-one basis. There were two 'Red Band' inmates who ran the bathing and clothing exchange unit in D Wing and I was to supervise them as the laundry was sorted, counted, itemised and transported by hand-drawn trailer-truck to the central unit. For some reason, the Wing Principal Officer involved himself in this process, walking over to where I stood watching the two orderlies sorting the dirty clothing into piles and counting them.

'Mr Sutton,' he interjected, 'Speed it up, you count the underpants.'

Well, I don't know if he really expected me to do that but, if he did, then the Wing Principal Officer was about to be disappointed. I just pointed at the two inmates doing the job.

'Not a chance,' I replied. 'Union rules,' and smiled at him but he didn't smile back.

The two orderlies burst out laughing; it seemed this was a joke they often played on new staff, getting them to sort through the prisoners' dirty undies to make them look foolish. I took a mental note of this incident, as there was a serious lesson to be learned here; it was that the senior staff and the inmates had a much more intimate understanding of each other than was immediately obvious.

That day, I had been scheduled a late shift; this entailed working through from 7am to 9pm at night. It was around 8:15pm and I was quite casually patrolling along D4 landing, when a prisoner I had met before called to me from his open cell.

'Hey! Mr Sutton, come have a look at this,' he shouted, so I went over to have a look at what he was indicating I should see.

To ensure I did not get locked into the cell, I shot the bolt on his cell door, gave the place a cursory glance and went in. There was a chair at the far end, below the iron-barred window, and it was to this that the inmate now directed me.

'Step up there and have a look; top row, four in from the right,' he said.

So, I thought, why not, stood on the chair and looked through the iron bars over the outer perimeter wall to the multi-story nurses' accommodation block of Hammersmith Hospital, which is located next to The Scrubs on the other side of Artillery Road. There were numerous windows illuminated and I could see directly into these. Following the inmate's advice, I looked at the top row and counted in four windows; the lights inside were full on and I could clearly see someone standing at an ironing board. Looking a little closer, I noted that this was a blonde-haired lady, completely naked and visible to well below the waist.

As I watched, she turned around and appeared to be staring through her window, across at the cells of D Wing, Wormwood Scrubs. Her dark pubic hair contrasted sharply with her pale skin and pink nipples. I nearly fell off that chair. The prisoner told me this was a regular exhibition and that particular nurse was not the only one flashing her minge at the inmates. It seemed a few of the female occupants of that accommodation block would parade naked at the windows, giving the long-term prisoners of D Wing a free show. (Some years later, it was reported in the press, that following complaints from Hammersmith Hospital staff, the remotely controlled security CCTV cameras attached to the perimeter walls of The Scrubs alongside Artillery Road had been fitted with restriction brackets, preventing them from being trained onto the nurses' accommodation block.)

Despite my good intentions to give up the booze and concentrate on my academic studies, I still had nights out with Paul C and our usual routine was to go for a Chinese meal after the shift, then hit the pubs. One night, it would have been around 7pm on a Thursday, we were in a respectable restaurant in Shepherd's Bush and had just ordered a meal. Our first beer was on the table before us and we were waiting to be served, when the door burst open and in ran two desperados, like Bonnie and Clyde. It was reminiscent of a scene from a Clint Eastwood-style movie, as they charged across the room and grabbed hold of a waiter by his neck. The manager came out and began to plead with them to let the little Chinese waiter go and asked what they wanted. It was what you might expect; all the money in the till and a takeaway meal, hilarious, I thought.

'On the count of three, you take the woman, I'll take the man.' I looked at Paul and he nodded. 'One…Two…Three,' and before the guy holding the hostage knew what was happening, I had smacked him in the nose, spun him round and run him face-first into the doorframe, before hurling him headlong into the street. A split second later, his girlfriend went flying past me and joined him on the pavement; they lay there looking totally bemused, obviously wondering what the hell had hit them. I just closed the door.

The waiter who had been half-strangled was weeping in relief and the manager just stood there in a kind of trance. The entire restaurant, which was about half full, stood up and cheered, clapping and shouting, 'Well done, lads.'

Paul and I just sat down and continued where we had left off but the manager was insisting we have the meal free on him.

'You save restaurant, very grateful,' he said again and again.

We tried to decline but he would not accept payment and even offered us a job protecting the place, which we respectfully refused; this was John and Paul, not Reggie and Ron.

The result of the Housing Committee meeting was published at the end of August and, as expected, I had not been allocated an apartment. But what was more disconcerting than that, neither had any of my fellow new recruits and some of these junior officers had been at The Scrubs for almost a year. There was no way I was going to manage twelve months separated from Mary; it had already been six months, taking the training school time into account, and I was starting to become somewhat perturbed. So, I went again to see the Chairman of the local branch of the Prison Officers' Association, the head of the housing committee, Principal Officer Mr B.

Or rather, I didn't, as this time, when I approached him, he refused to speak to me, claiming he was too busy. This man, Principal Officer Mr B, was the most senior member of the local branch of the trade union, the POA I was paying subscriptions to, expecting representation to support me. He was also a senior member of the prison management team, being the Principal Officer in charge of the entire prison rota, which meant he allocated all the discipline staff, including me, their shifts. No wonder he was too busy to see me.

At this point, I began to realise that, as far as representation was concerned, there was only one man who was going to represent me and I was him, which is exactly what I decided to set about doing, but how?

I woke in the middle of the night in my lodgings on Carlisle Avenue with a vision in my mind, as if I had been shown something in the dream and this was, I knew, of great importance. In my vision, I had seen a number of empty houses, empty rooms and no one there, row upon row of unoccupied properties. Suddenly, I was wide awake. Perhaps that was the message; it could be that there were many empty apartments and houses available for allocation at HMP Wormwood Scrubs but, for some reason, they were not being allocated to newly-recruited junior staff. I could not get back to sleep; there had to be a way for me to find out exactly what the total housing stock of The Scrubs was. I also needed to know exactly the total number of properties that were currently unoccupied. The vision had come to me for a purpose; now I had to do something about it.

The next day, I went to speak to a number of the junior staff who, like myself, were waiting to be housed, in accordance with the terms of our contract of employment. I arranged a meeting one lunchtime, at which around fifteen of the newly-appointed officers sat down with me and we discussed how to find out the exact number of houses available. One officer advised that his uncle was a Senior Officer in the Works Department at The Scrubs and he would ask him. The Works Department was responsible for the maintenance of all housing quarters, so he would know not only how many units there were, but also how many were standing empty. He could, he said, get the answer to us pretty quickly, as his uncle was on duty that week. Then, what would we do? I wanted the information first, then I could formulate a plan for the next phase. We all agreed to meet in a week's time to discuss this and I asked them to please say nothing to anyone else. I suspected the established order of control would not look too kindly on junior staff questioning their authority.

CHAPTER 10

WHERE ANGELS FEAR TO TREAD

It was a hot Saturday morning in early September and I was on duty in C Wing, supervising the inmates working on the hot-plates, serving the meals. It would have been around 11am; the majority of the wing's inmates were out on the exercise yard, enjoying a pleasant stroll under an almost cloudless sky. As I walked along C1 landing, I passed an open cell and happened to look in where, to my utter amazement, I saw a prisoner dressed in the outfit of a church choir boy. There was no way under prison rules that this inmate could lawfully have these vestments in his cell; they belonged in the prison chapel.

Pushing the cell door open wide, I shot the bolt, walked in and asked this inmate what on earth he thought he was playing at. He was a relatively young man; I estimated his age as around twenty-two or three. He was trembling and crying as I spoke to him and this was not my doing, as I was not unduly harsh. I did, however, require him to explain why and how he came to be dressed up like a choir boy, when he should have been outside, taking exercise with everyone else. The tears continued from this young man and I suggested he sit down on his bed, calm down and tell me the truth.

For a few moments, the sobbing continued but gradually, when he realised I was not going hurt him, he started to splutter out his story. He was, he said, a member of the church choir and this was his surplice that he wore during the Sunday service, at which he sang. I advised that, yes, I could accept that but how and why did he have this outfit in his cell when he knew perfectly well that it was strictly forbidden? The tears started again.

'Boss, I can't tell you, Boss, I can't,' he was sobbing and stuttering, tears streaming down his face. I have never been a tactile individual, unless I connect with force, that is, but I put my hand on his shoulder to comfort him and advised that he could tell me or The Governor.

The story this young man now told me was seriously disturbing and caused me to wonder what I should do next. He said that, during his time practicing with the choir in the prison chapel, he had come into contact with a member of the clergy, who had persuaded him to engage in certain homosexual acts. One of these acts involved this young man, dressed as a choir boy, getting down on his hands and knees, then performing fellatio on the clergyman, whom he named. It had, the young man continued, become the practice of this clergyman to visit him in his cell during the Saturday morning exercise period and, always, he had to dress as a choir boy before indulging said clergyman by sucking his penis and, he said, he was forced to swallow his ejaculated sperm.

'Don't tell anyone, please, promise me you won't,' he cried, bursting into tears again.

I knew what I had to do and it wasn't going to be easy. I told the prisoner to remove the surplice, which I placed in a pillowcase, then I got a sheet of A4 paper from the wing office and took his statement, which I asked him to sign. I kept it simple and used his words as best I could, making sure he agreed that what I wrote down for him was a true account of what had transpired. He was still weeping when I took him to the Hospital Officer's clinic and asked him to take care of the young man, while I dealt with another matter.

Having written my report on A4 paper, I copied it out again, so I had my own copy and duly signed it. Then, along with the prisoner's signed statement and the choir boy's surplice, I went to see the C Wing Principal Officer. I gave him a brief summary of what had happened and showed him the choir boy's outfit, told him I had a statement from the inmate and had written my own. To say that my report was not received with great enthusiasm would be a massive understatement; the P.O. looked thunder-struck. He said nothing at all to me, picked up the telephone and spoke to someone, replaced the handset then pointed at the door.

'Number One Chief Officer NOW!' he shouted. I sensed he was not best pleased with my diligent application to duty.

The most senior uniformed Discipline grade in any of Her Majesty's Prisons is, or was at the time, the Number One Chief Prison Officer. At The Scrubs, this man was CO1 Mr G and his office was located in the main office block, which was where I was now heading, clutching my two written statements and the supporting evidence. I knocked on the door of the CO1 and a booming great voice shouted, 'Come in.'

He was enormous: bulging chest, twenty-inch neck, mighty fists that I noticed were clenched and he appeared leaning forward almost seated on the edge of his chair behind his civil service issue desk, wearing the full regalia of a Number One Chief Officer of HM Prisons, rather like a Japanese Admiral, all gold braid, silver insignia and a big shiny hat.

'Mr Sutton, Sir, you are expecting me?' I ventured.

What looked much like steam seemed to be hissing from his ears as this gigantic man glared at me. I lifted the choir boy's surplice from the pillowcase and passed it to him, as I briefly explained what had taken place. As I did so, I noticed his complexion seemed to be changing from slightly red to deep puce and his eyes were wild, flickering open then closed; then he jumped up and thumped the desk so hard, it near split in half.

'Who authorised you to investigate senior staff members of this prison!' he growled at me. 'I have known this man for years; how dare you Mr Sutton, HOW DARE YOU!'.

I handed over the two statements and did my best to quietly explain that, on my Prison Officer's Warrant Card, it said that under the Prison Act 1953 Section 8 'Every Prison Officer, while acting as such, shall have all the power, authority, protection and privileges of a Constable.' I was, I attempted to assure the CO1, simply carrying out my duties and that he, as my most senior manager in uniform, was obliged under the Prison Act 1953 to assist me in so doing.

'GET OUT!....GET OUT OF THIS OFFICE NOW!'

I was gradually becoming accustomed to being told to exit offices.

My recent encounters with the supernatural in The Scrubs had got me thinking about the paranormal and communications from beyond the veil. Mary had been to see a professional psychic in Leigh and I recalled her account of the dire predictions made. Perhaps now these were coming true, as I seemed to be always getting involved in difficult situations. Given that and the fact I had started to witness inexplicable phenomena, such as the levitating beds and the ghost of D Wing, I thought it was perhaps time for me to look a little deeper into the subject. In the town of Acton, just a mile or so from my lodgings, there was a Spiritualist Church and my landlady told me it was the best place to go if I was seriously interested in contacting the spirit world. I checked the church out and found that, on Sunday evenings, they held a service starting at 6:30pm. I decided to attend.

The building in which Acton Spiritualist Church held its services was more functional than impressive, rather like a village hall. I took a seat towards the rear of the congregation and attempted to appear as inconspicuous as possible. I was mainly interested in seeing what this was all about, as I had never been into such a church before. I knew that, in my family, a Great Aunt had been a Spiritualist, but no one spoke much of her. My father had been a practising member of The Roman Catholic Church, so the subject of Spiritualism was taboo in our house.

As the service began, I instantly felt at ease; the minister, a lady in late middle age, addressed us all, speaking of healing the sick and asking for prayers to help absent members. Then we all sang a hymn and, really, this service seemed much like those conducted in the Church of England, into which I had been confirmed. Then, after further mention of forthcoming meetings, the Spiritualist minister introduced to the platform an elderly lady dressed all in black, with silver hair and an angelic appearance. I was instantly mesmerised, looking at her; she seemed to shine a deep shade of blue, flickering, illuminating the podium where she stood staring out. She was staring directly at me.

'Young man at the back of the room.' She spoke so gently, pointing straight at me. 'You have a father figure in spirit with you. His name is Frank,' she said.

I was shocked, as Frank was my father and he had died some two years ago.

'Yes,' I replied, trying to stay calm but secretly shaking in my boots.

'He says you are in uniform, he shows me himself dressed as a policeman, you know this Spirit?'

Her words caused a strange, almost uncontrollable emotion within me and tears came to my eyes.

'I do, that is my father,' I replied and my voice trembled as I spoke.

'Though you walk through the valley of the shadow of death, you must fear no evil, for he is with you, John, he is by your side,' she said.

By now I was crying; how did she know my name was John, how could she know?

'Thank you, dear lady,' I said, mumbling the words through my tears.

Then she made a sign as if to bless me and began speaking to another member of the congregation. I walked out of Acton Spiritualist Church in a kind of dream, my mind full of the wonder of that incredible communication.

The next day, I was back on duty, when the officer with the uncle in the Works Department came to see me on C Wing. He told me he had the information regarding the housing stock at HMP Wormwood Scrubs. The exact details are lost in the mists of time, but I recall that there were more unoccupied properties available than there were junior officers on the waiting list. Why, I wondered, were the housing committee not offering these to staff, some of whom had been on the waiting list for over twelve months? I thanked my colleague and began to consider how I could best use the information he had provided me with. It didn't take me long to come up with a plan; I would once more approach the chairman of the housing committee and demand an explanation. Then, depending on what he said, I would decide how to proceed.

Principal Officer Mr B agreed to spare me some of his valuable time and invited me into his office, where he listened to what I had to say. Why, I asked him, were there over twenty properties empty, when they could be allocated to newly-appointed staff, who were entitled under the terms of their contract to housing. The PO gave me a rather amused stare and offered as explanation an idea that these properties were being prepared for incoming senior staff from other London establishments, such as HMP Wandsworth and HMP Pentonville, etc. It was, in my opinion, a totally unacceptable explanation, but I thanked PO Mr B and said I would consider what he said. Which I did do; I did consider that what he had told me was tantamount to an insult and I was determined to do something about it.

I checked in the Home Office rules and regulations governing the provision of accommodation to Prison Staff and found that the actual responsibility for the housing stock of any establishment resided entirely with The Governor. The Housing Committee were, in effect, appointed by The Governor to manage the housing accommodation on his behalf. That meant I had another avenue of approach, direct to the Number One Governor of HMP Wormwood Scrubs. I had a list of all the officers waiting for housing at The Scrubs and I decided to approach them, with a view to taking direct action.

My idea was to present The Governor with a petition, signed by all interested staff, and demand that he, as the government official responsible for the housing stock, intervene with the Housing Committee he had appointed and ensure that all entitled officers were housed. I wrote out the heading of the petition, addressing it to The Governor, and placed my own name at the top, then signed it. There followed a tour of the jail, as I went round to the junior staff involved, asking them to add their names. Some declined, as they did not want to associate themselves with what was certain to be trouble, but most agreed. At the end of two days, I had twelve or so signatures. I went into the main office and knocked on the Number One Chief Officer's door. When he saw who it was that had the nerve to enter his domain, he near choked on his coffee. Then, when I told him I needed to see The Governor, he began to shake with barely controlled anger. But I was within my rights to ask to see The Governor and so it was, the CO1 Mr G accompanied me to the main man's office.

The Number One Governor of HMP Wormwood Scrubs was Mr H; he was of late middle age, a gentleman of slight stature, with a rather academic appearance. Staring over his glasses, Mr H listened as I advised him why I needed to see him, to present the petition from his newly-appointed prison officers. I sensed immediately that this man had absolutely no idea whatsoever what the housing committee were doing in his name. I carefully and politely pointed out that, as The Governor, he had the absolute authority to allocate the housing stock available to any officer serving at his establishment. Then I detailed the available stock and advised exactly what the Chairman of his housing committee had told me.

The CO1 Mr G attempted to interject with some bluster about protocol and I saw that The Governor was listening a little too closely to his argument. It was time to do something drastic or face being given the brush-off and it would all have been a waste of time.

'The officers on the petition have been waiting long enough for the accommodation they were promised when they joined The Prison Service,' I said, feeling it was now or never. 'In the event that the available housing is not released and allocated immediately, then they, along with myself, will be demonstrating outside this jail, with placards demanding our rights and I know the press will love that.'

Mr H just sat behind his desk staring at me, while to his immediate right, the CO1 stood, clenching and unclenching his fists. I did not need to be told it was time to go, thanked The Governor for seeing me and beat a hasty retreat before CO1 Mr G could get his mighty mitts on me.

It was now September and I had started the Sociology diploma course at Ealing College. The first module was on social history, starting with the industrial revolution, and it really took my mind off The Scrubs. Our lecturer was David Kidd-Hewitt; he seemed to find it interesting that a jailer had joined his class, as the other students were mainly female office workers, looking for a new direction. There were numerous essays to complete and a lot of reading; it was just what I needed after plodding the landings, slopping out the inmates of C2 and banging them up. The only problem was getting the time off to attend and the only way I could do that was to swap my late shifts when they fell on a Thursday.

I was collecting C Wing's meals from the central cookhouse with my two orderlies, when I met up with Paul C. He told me the Housing Committee had just published a list of houses and apartments available for entitled applicants. He seemed quite surprised and said that something must have happened, as there were at least ten properties listed. Maybe my meeting with The Governor had shaken them up; I believed it must have done. That lunchtime in the prison club, I was joined by many of the newly-appointed staff, those who had signed my petition and many who had not; they too were applying for the listed apartments and houses. There was a real sense of excitement that maybe now we would all get the accommodation we were entitled to, for ourselves and our families. Now I had to go get the forms filled in and submit my application. That night, I telephoned Mary and told her I had applied for a number of apartments and actually believed that this time, I was going to be successful. A silent voice in my mind told me that soon she would be with me in London.

The results of the Housing Committee meeting were due to

be published some three weeks after the closing date and it was now early October. All the new staff, including me, were anxiously waiting to see if we had a place to live. Paul C had not applied; he wanted to be transferred from The Scrubs to HMP Liverpool at Walton Jail, as his wife had decided she wouldn't move to London. He was still living in his lodgings on Goldhawk Road but Paul was not happy there; it seemed the landlady seriously objected to the smell of his sweaty socks and kept warning him to have his laundry done. Paul's problem was that he spent most of his spare time in the boozer and, being almost constantly under the influence, he did not realise how pungent his clothing had become, especially his socks.

I had called in on him one Saturday evening after my shift had finished, to see if he fancied a meal out and a beer, of course. The formidable landlady opened the door of her house and invited me in, pointing down a hallway.

She said, 'Follow your nose, the pig is in the end room.'

When I knocked on Paul's door, he shouted, 'Come in.'

I did and was near knocked over by the revolting stench of unwashed sweaty clothing. Paul was flopped out on his bed, swigging lager from an open can. In the middle of the room, there stood a large green plastic dustbin that was filled with soggy clothes.

'She's given me till tomorrow to get rid of the smelly socks, etc, or she's throwing me out.'

We spent the next few hours at the launderette in Acton and those clothes took some washing. Quite how he had managed to get himself into such a state, I will never know; maybe he was just always too drunk to bother. By 9pm, I had managed to get all his laundry washed and tumbled dry. I also bought a jumbo-size air freshener spay and some bars of perfumed soap. Paul was not too delighted at what he saw as a waste of his good boozing money but, if I had not intervened and insisted he clean up, then into the street he would have been thrown.

On the day the list of successful applicants for housing was published on the POA notice board at The Scrubs, I was suddenly surrounded by junior staff, who were all anxious to congratulate me on getting an apartment. I went with them to check that this was for real and, sure enough, there was my name, Officer John Sutton: 118 Bromyard Avenue. To say that I was delighted did not come close; I was so pleased, I just had to go and telephone Mary immediately. But the other staff wouldn't let me; they wanted to know how I had done it, when their applications had failed. It seemed that the majority of the properties allocated from the list of ten or so had gone to more senior staff, joining The Scrubs from other London prisons.

'How did you do it, John?' they asked, obviously disappointed.

I knew how. 'You get a petition up and put your name on the top, then you go see The Number One Governor and tell him, unless you get a property at the next meeting of the housing committee, you will lead a demonstration outside the gates of his prison.'

CHAPTER 11

PARAFFIN LAMPS

Paul C insisted we go out and celebrate my success in being allocated a prison quarter; that meant hitting the boozers as soon as we were changed out of uniform. I called Mary from the Askew Arms public house and told her the fantastic news. We had been separated for more than seven months, but it felt like ages to me and I knew she was seriously fed up, being alone in our one-bedroom flat on St. Helens Road in Leigh, Lancashire.

'When can we move in, John?' she asked and I had already posed that question at The Scrubs.

'The keys will be in my hands tomorrow, so get packing, Mary.'

It was an exciting moment telling my wife that, at last, after all this time, we would be together again.

'Your round,' said Paul as I went back into the bar, where he was ordering our third pint of beer and it was not yet 7pm.

We ended up in a right dive of a boozer, somewhere in the middle of Shepherd's Bush. I had lost track of time and the number of beers we had taken on board. The public house we were in was full of Irish workmen, singing and shouting at each other as the Guinness flowed fast. At one point, there was a collection made by a huge bloke wearing a black beret and balaclava; he did not say it was to support the IRA but that was quite obvious, as the entire pub was singing a rebel song, 'Kevin Barry'.

Paul and I donated a few coins. If this lot only knew that we were locking their heroes up in The Scrubs, then they would no doubt have attacked us. As it was, we sat down and sang along, pouring more and more beer in, as the room began to rotate. I barely remember the Chinese restaurant we found ourselves in after the pubs had closed, but I do recall Paul collapsing on the pavement outside and vomiting all over the place. I was just about capable of hailing a taxi, but the driver was reluctant to take Paul, as he was so totally pissed. You could see that by the way he was flopped out in the gutter at the side of the road. Inside the cab, I had forgotten where we lived, so had to direct the driver to take us to The Scrubs. From there, I knew my way, but it was a really horrible feeling, being stoned and lost in London, trying to locate my lodgings with a snoring drunken Paul on the cab floor.

It must have been around 4am when I woke, completely naked, from a deep drunken sleep, in a place I did not recognise. Who had stolen my clothes? There was, in my mind, a vague recollection of coming in through a door, but in the total pitch black night, I now could not find it. Someone had moved the entrance while I was asleep, I knew they had, and now there was no way out. I had a seriously urgent need to urinate; it was already starting to dribble down my leg. I began moving along the wall, searching for a way out. I finally found the door, somehow managed to open it and, gripping my penis in my hand to stop it squirting everywhere, I stumbled on to the landing and turned left into what I believed to be the bathroom. It wasn't.

'Wrong room, John!' screamed my little old landlady, shining a torchlight in my eyes, and looking down, I could see she was right.

But where was the toilet? Staggering out of her bedroom, I crashed into the banister at the top of the stairs, down which I almost fell, rebounded and grabbed the door handle to the bathroom, except I was wrong again. I wasn't having much luck really, as the room in which I now found myself, dick in hand, was occupied by the landlady's eighty-two-year-old brother who, if memory serves me well, looked absolutely terrified. The last thing I recall was climbing into a wardrobe that I had mistaken for the loo. I thought it was a bit small, then I released the grip on my willy and mercifully pissed myself to sleep. And that is where the landlady discovered me the next morning, naked, dripping wet through with urine, wrapped up in her brother's piss-soaked suit, half hanging out of the wardrobe.

There was a deadly silence as I went to apologise to my elderly landlady and her older brother. To my eternal shame, I was ordered to pack my things and exit Carlisle Avenue immediately. I just piled my suitcase and everything else in the back of the beaten-up old Hillman Imp I had bought to replace my smashed-up MGB and, hanging my head in disgrace, I drove off to start my shift at The Scrubs.

Amazingly, I was not late, unlike my boozing buddy Paul, who had taken the day off sick, as I discovered when I enquired about him on B Wing. His digs were not that far away so, to make sure he was OK, I called in to see him during my lunch break. His landlady actually smiled at me and again pointed down the hallway.

'The pig is in there,' she grumbled.

When I told Paul about my experience in the wardrobe, he nearly fell out of bed laughing. I looked a little closer at the man and noticed his shoes poking out from under the sheets. He was fully dressed; no wonder his clothing stank, as he was obviously in the habit of climbing into his pit, fully clothed.

With the keys in my pocket to the apartment I had been allocated, I set off in the Hillman to drive the two hundred or so miles to Leigh in Lancashire and Mary. It was Friday evening and the traffic was bumper to bumper all the way to the M1, and I was somewhat irritable, having decided to quit smoking. For the past ten years or so, I had been hooked on cigarettes, smoking around forty a day of the powerful coffin nails they called Benson and Hedges. It was proving to be an expensive habit and one that was making me ill.

Recently, I had noticed that each morning, I woke coughing and the only thing that eased this was a ciggie. Also, I was becoming a little breathless when ascending the steep metal stairs in the jail and, at just twenty-six years of age, that was, I felt, a sure sign that something was wrong. Forty fags a day was what was wrong, so I had stopped, gone cold turkey with a half full pack of Benson and Hedges in my pocket. I had quit. Now I had to drive for around four hours without a cigarette and it was tough, but I simply had to stop smoking. Every time I felt like lighting a fag, I took the packet out of my pocket and shouted abuse at the damn nicotine sticks.

'You bastards, you stinking rotten little bastards won't get me!' I yelled as I edged the car forward, heading for the motorway and home.

Mary was waiting for me when I walked in the back door of our little flat. She had prepared a meal for us and, together, we sat at our old-fashioned kitchen table, took a glass of wine over the late supper and stared at those magnificent keys. We were moving on now; I had what I thought of as a regular job, steady money, somewhere to live and I was studying on an accredited London University course. The next thing we had to do was arrange the transportation of our belongings and household goods to our new home and move in.

This was to be through the company Pickfords and Co, paid for by The Home Office, as part of my entitlement. I had already got the contact details of Pickfords and would be calling them first thing Monday morning, to arrange an early removal to London. We had so many hopes for our future together; I recall Mary saying she wanted some new furniture, a new fridge and so forth. But most of all, what we both wanted was a child; we were in our sixth year of marriage and it was time. There was no reason we knew of as to why Mary had not conceived; at no point in our married life had we taken precautions. I remember discussing this with Mary that long ago weekend in October of 1975 and we both agreed that, when the moment was right, it would happen. I knew it would not be long. For some weeks, I had been having vivid dreams of a child in Mary's arms; in those dreams, I kept hearing the same nursery rhyme: 'Twinkle Twinkle Little Star, How I Wonder What You Are'.

Back at The Scrubs, I decided to move myself into our new

apartment using a sleeping bag, since I had nowhere else to stay, having been thrown out of my lodgings. It was number 118 Bromyard Avenue, a two-storey apartment, in the centre of a three-block set of housing units, connected by a central walkway. The entrance was by stairs, leading up from the main walkway into the building along a corridor and 118 was located at the far end. It consisted of an entrance hall, kitchen on the left, stairs up to the next storey, a main lounge with a small balcony to the front through opening glass doors, two bedrooms and a bathroom upstairs. I slept in the main bedroom on the bare floor, as there were no carpets. It was cold, it was lonely but it wasn't for long, as Pickfords had agreed to expedite our removal. Meanwhile, I continued with my duties on C Wing, walking in each morning, alongside the many other prison staff who also lived on Bromyard Avenue.

There was a strange routine on C Wing that, to me, seemed really disturbing. On the first landing, known as C1, certain cells, directly opposite the shower units, had been designated for what the landing officers called 'Paraffin Lamps'; that is, cockney rhyming slang for tramps. I had previously been detailed to supervise the cleaning of these cells and deal with the occupants, I recalled that horrible experience.

These unfortunate inmates usually appeared on Friday evenings, direct from court, having been lifted by the police, in an attempt to clear central London of their unwanted presence at the weekend. The problem with these rough-sleeping homeless prisoners was that they were, as a general rule, filthy, infested with lice and stank of human excrement. Some were doubly incontinent and, by rights, should have been cared for in a nursing home, except nowhere would have them. So, the courts threw them into jail and they ended up on C1 landing at The Scrubs.

The practice was, on a Saturday morning, before unlocking the rest of the wing, the occupants of these cells would be forcibly dragged out, thrown into the shower unit opposite the cells, then hosed down with the fire hose. Now, this was a really powerful fire hose and it blasted the 'Paraffin Lamps', fully dressed as they were, from one side of the shower unit to the other. Then, once they were fully soaked, their clothing was removed by the landing cleaners and they were hosed down again with freezing cold water. No one wanted to touch these unfortunates, as they were often crawling with lice and fleas.

One of them, I saw, had hair that was set into a kind of hard helmet, so congealed with grime, dirt and detritus was it. Another had, believe this or not, toe nails that had grown through the sides of his boots and curled round the front like a toe cap. Once they had been forcibly doused, the poor people were dragged out of the showers naked and thrown back into their cells which, while they were being hosed, had been given a clean out by other trusted inmates in the cleaning team. It was a vision of hell from the days of Bedlam to witness this disgraceful exhibition on a Saturday morning.

Also on a Saturday mornings, directly after breakfast was completed, there was the task of allocating cells to the new intake of prisoners from the courts, who had arrived late on Friday. One particular day, I was given the job of locating the prisoners, which could only be done one at a time, according to availability of cells on C Wing and the place was operating at near capacity. So, I asked all the landing senior officers to supply me with their cell availability and set about allocating the inmates to the places, then reporting their location to the central senior officer. This was a time-consuming task and, as I did this, I had all last night's new admissions lined up on C1 landing, directly opposite the main office unit that had a forward-facing open window, at which the senior officer was seated. I was doing my best to get all the prisoners located, sorting this a landing at a time, when out of the ranks came a prisoner, who spoke to me in a manner to which I was not accustomed.

'I say, get a move on, my good fellow, I have been here half the damn morning, you know.'

For a moment, I honestly thought he was joking. I couldn't

believe that any inmate would be so bold as to challenge a member of staff, going about the commission of their duties. But no, this certain inmate was standing his ground and appeared to think he had a valid point. Now, in prison, there has to be good order and discipline; inmates must know who is in charge or there would quickly be chaos, as at any given time, there could be four hundred prisoners and just around forty staff on duty. So, if the inmates had even a moment of doubt about who was in command, there could be serious trouble. Obviously, I had to deal with this rather open affront to my authority and I knew exactly what to do.

'You are clearly not satisfied with the service I am providing, so go to that window there and make a formal complaint about me to my senior officer.'

You, dear reader, may think, how understanding of Mr Sutton to listen to that inmate's complaint and allow him to make a direct approach to a more senior member of staff and register his dissatisfaction with the performance of my duties. So you might well think, but this was not a branch of The General Post Office, this was The Scrubs. The senior officer sitting behind that window was a well-known maniac who, prior to joining Her Majesty's Prison Service, had been an internationally famous professional wrestler and he was not a man to mess with.

As the prisoner crossed the landing and walked up to the window, I held my breath. Quite what he said I could not hear, but it certainly got the attention of the SO.

'Mr Sutton!' he shouted and I made haste to attend. 'Put this prisoner in with the paraffin lamps.'

Without hesitation, I guided that inmate along C1 landing, opened a cell opposite the showers, placed his card outside the door and helped him inside, to join two incontinent tramps. The place stank like a fractured sewer. There was a look of absolute terror on his face as I went to close the door, which I did. I then returned to my duties and continued allocating the rest of the new intake to their cells. There were no further complaints.

I was having a coffee in the officers' Kardomah café unit on C1, when in came the SO from the central wing office. He seemed highly amused at what had happened to that foolish prisoner and asked if I knew who he was. Of course, I had absolutely no idea who the man might be; he was to me just another inmate that I had to deal with, in accordance with my duties. It seemed, the SO advised me, that the prisoner was in fact a Formula One racing driver who had been sentenced for killing a pedestrian, while driving his Ferrari drunk, in the centre of London. It was, so he told me, the second time that man had killed someone, while intoxicated behind the wheel.

He was laughing about how racing boy would enjoy meeting his new friends, when we heard the sound of running feet. We were up and out of the café unit in under a second and looked down the landing, to see the subject of our conversation being dragged out of his cell and physically restrained by a number of strong staff. We went over to see what the problem was; it seemed that this prisoner had been banging and thumping on his cell door, while at the same time screaming the place down. He was now being forcibly restrained on the floor by three big jailers, who had no problem holding him still, but the screaming; well, he continued that all the way out of the wing, despite being strapped onto a stretcher en-route to the hospital unit and a nice clean padded cell.

CHAPTER 12

MEETING THE LOCAL LOUTS

It was November 1975 and we had moved into our prison quarter on Bromyard Avenue, Acton, London W12. The apartment was quite spacious, certainly a lot more room than we had in our one-bedroom flat in Leigh. Mary's dog, a little Jack Russell terrier she called Snowy, soon found a favourite spot and made herself at home. The dog had kept Mary company all these months we had been separated and, despite the fact she was an ankle biter, Snowy was a good pet. Useless as a guard dog, she would welcome anyone, but getting out was another matter altogether; she hated people leaving and attacked their ankles, mine included.

There were plenty trees along Bromyard Avenue and, pretty soon, Snowy had christened them all, as I took her for a walk there each evening, after my shift at The Scrubs. So here we were in London and I was earning a living; I had even bought a house from my grandparents and was paying them for this each month. It wasn't a big property, just the small two-up-two-down 17th century cottage they had owned, next door to their home in the little village of Foulridge in Lancashire. We couldn't even use it for long weekends, though, as it was still rented out to a long-term tenant, an old lady who had been in there years. But, I reasoned, this was a house and, in time, it would serve its purpose for us. That was part of our plan, anyway, and it seemed to make sense at the time, as it provided my maternal grandparents money and it gave me some longer term security.

We had been in the apartment no more than a fortnight and things were settling down well, or so it seemed at the time. I walked to and from The Scrubs to my work and back, a distance of around half a mile or so. Mary had found her way around the local shops and was happy enough going into Acton town centre at the weekend. I had been doing quite a lot of overtime, extra late shifts to get some money in for Christmas and I was still not smoking, so we saved on that expense.

Then one night, it would have been around 8pm, I heard a lot of shouting from the area immediately below the opposite block of apartments. It sounded like abuse to me, being yelled at someone, so I opened the balcony door and walked out, looking down and across the open grassed land to the driveway and car park underneath the apartments opposite. There, I saw a group of four or five young men, standing around and shouting up at someone in one of the apartments above them.

What they were yelling to them was deeply disturbing: 'We know your husband's away on a course, Mrs. We'll come up and give you a good fucking.'

I called Mary over to look at this gang of louts and asked her if she had seen them before. Indeed she had. Mary told me that, most nights, this group of young men would be hanging around the outside area, shouting insults to the women and generally making a nuisance of themselves. It took me less than a minute to put the lead on Snowy the dog, grab a coat and head out of our apartment to have a word with these yobbos.

The gang of louts was still there, leaning against the concrete supports by the car park beneath the apartment block. There were five of them, tall young men, aged sixteen to eighteen, casually dressed in jeans and woollen jumpers, smoking and generally looking like trouble. Being as diplomatic as I could be, I asked the biggest of the gang his name.

He answered me in an insolent tone. 'I'm LB and my father is your boss, so piss off with your dumb dog, arsehole.'

His little troop of hangers-on laughed at that remark and one flicked his cigarette butt at little Snowy. As I said, I was being diplomatic, so as gently as I could, given the circumstances, I advised LB and his buddies that, if I ever saw them around the area again, I would be going to see their parents. For some reason, that seemed to amuse them.

'Fuck off, you silly cunt, they know where we are, we can do what we want and my father will just tell you the same.' said LB, who was obviously the ring leader.

By this time, my sangfroid was starting to slip, allowing the darker side of my nature to materialise. They must have sensed danger as I stepped closer to them and pointed at the way out of the complex, as they moved back and began walking away.

'You're a cunt,' shouted LB loudly and his voice bounced off the buildings, echoing all around the complex, but no one came out to see what was going on and they must have heard.

In my heart, I knew then why this gang of louts dared to do what they were doing, abusing the occupants of these prison quarters. The leader of the yobs was the son of Principal Officer Mr B. He was the Chairman of the POA. and of The Housing Committee, as well as being in charge of the prison staff rota. I decided I needed a word with this man, as there was no way I could tolerate a bunch of teenage hoods, terrorising and torment-ing the innocent residents of the housing complex I was living in.

The next day at The Scrubs, I made some enquiries and found the home address of PO Mr B. He lived some few hundred yards away from Bromyard Avenue in a semi-detached house, which was also a prison quarter. I spoke to Mary that evening and asked her what she thought of my idea of going round to see Mr B and advising him of exactly what his son was getting up to. Both Mary and I were optimistic that Mr B would accept that such loutish behaviour was unacceptable and advise his boy to stay clear of the Bromyard Avenue housing area. So, around 7pm that night, I walked round to the home of Mr B and knocked on his front door.

The door was opened by Mr B himself and he looked most surprised to see me, but he did invite me in and we stood just inside his hallway, facing each other. There followed a strange, strained conversation, as I explained to him that, the previous evening, his son LB and a group of other young men had been hanging round the Bromyard Avenue housing area, shouting abuse at the wives of officers who lived there. I was quite explicit and gave Mr B a detailed account of what had transpired and, furthermore, that my enquiries had led me to believe that this kind of nonsense had been going on for some time.

I then explained quite clearly that, as from now, such behaviour would not be tolerated and he should advise his son LB to stay away from the officers' quarters, as he did not live there and had no legitimate reason for being in that area. I did point out that LB was on the road to perdition and, as a father, he surely did not want that for his son. My observations and comments were not, however, accepted in the spirit in which they were given and Mr B took it upon himself to issue me with a warning.

'My son is free to go where he wants, he can do what he wants and, Mr Sutton, if you so much as lay a finger on him, I will have you in court, now get out!'

For a moment, I was thunderstruck. This man was the parent of a young man, who was walking down a dark and dangerous path. I had taken my time to come and caution him that he should act to prevent his boy from meeting an inevitable sticky end.

'Mr B,' I replied, 'there is going to be trouble.'

And with that, I turned and left. As I did so, a weird sensation came over me; it was as if I had seen all this before and what had just happened had happened before. I also heard a silent voice in my mind speaking my name: 'John….John…..John!' It was the voice of my late father and the tone was one of alarm.

On duty in The Scrubs, I found myself on a Home Office production, taking an inmate to visit his wife, who was serving a prison sentence in HMP Holloway. For this escort, I was paired up with my boozing buddy Paul C, so it promised to be an enjoyable experience, despite the fact we were going to another Victorian jail. The prisoner was no trouble and had made this journey a number of times, so he knew to behave himself and all would be peaceful.

Holloway jail was built in 1852 as a male and female prison, with one notable male inmate being Oscar Wilde. In 1903, it became exclusively a female prison. It was at Holloway that the last woman to be executed in Great Britain was hung by Albert Pierrepoint, the hangman. She was Ruth Ellis, whose mortal remains were interred in an unmarked grave within the prison walls. We were travelling by taxi, a fairly common way of transporting inmates not considered to be exceptionally dangerous. At the gates of Holloway, we knocked on the gate and were admitted to a family visitors' unit, where we handed our prisoner over to the Holloway staff and agreed a time to collect him. The senior officer there, a tall hefty blonde lady with close-cut hair, suggested we take a break in the staff club just outside the main gates and return after lunch. This seemed a great idea.

Paul and I were soon enjoying a beer in the Holloway Officers' Club and the female jailers in there made us welcome. I did notice one or two of the staff looked overtly glamorous, more like Hollywood starlets than Holloway jailers. These platinum blonde beauties were obviously spoken for and closely accompanied by androgynous muscular partners with hands like hams. I recall chatting to one lady, who told me her husband was a Principal Officer at Wormwood Scrubs and I had met him. I asked her what it was like working there and she pointed out to me a smartly-dressed middle-aged woman in a pin-striped suit with shiny shoes, old school tie and immaculately dressed. 'She's one of the Governors.' It did not seem possible.

Paul was entertaining himself, swigging beer and eating pies; he had quite an appetite for meat and potato pasties. After about three pints, Paul decided to have a wander round, so I sat alone quietly, with that day's copy of The Daily Telegraph crossword, not paying much attention. I was suddenly disturbed from my contemplations by the unmistakeable sound of a brawl. There were loud female screams and the sound of breaking glass, followed by a series of deep thumping thuds, as if someone was pounding a wall. Then Paul arrived rather rapidly, looking distinctly dishevelled, his hair was all over the place; he had a busted top lip dripping blood and, on his face, were two long red scratch marks.

'Let's get out of here,' he shouted, picked his hat up and we both headed with great haste for the exit.

Outside the Holloway Prison Officers' Club, Paul told me what had happened. It seemed he had walked to the far side of the premises and saw a slot machine there; I know them as One-Armed Bandits. He had put some money in, pulled the handle and, much to his surprise, won the jackpot of around twenty pounds or so. Delighted with this, he was just pocketing his winnings when an enormous female jailer had grabbed his arm and demanded half of the cash.

Now, Paul was a big man, I would say fifteen stone and six foot or so, a substantial presence. He said when he resisted the woman and told her no chance, she had begun shouting that she was due at least half, as Paul had jumped on the machine she was playing, when she went to get change. That didn't impress Paul, but the smack in the mouth he received next got his attention. This was followed by two fingers with sharp nails raking at his face and he had to fight back or risk being injured by this wild woman jailer. As I said Paul was a big lad, so when his attempt to restrain her reasonably had no effect, he had just punched the mad bitch twice and run for it. That would have been the two loud thuds I had heard, immediately before he arrived back at my table. In his hurry to escape, Paul had abandoned at least half his winnings so, in a way, that crazy female jailer had got her money. I made a mental note never to go anywhere near the Officers' Club at any female prison ever again.

It was late November and I was patrolling C2 landing at The Scrubs, when I heard a disturbance in a cell, so opened the door to see what was going on. At first, I thought I was seeing things; there was what appeared to be a woman in a patterned dress, kneeling down in front of two prisoners, who were rubbing their erect penises into 'her' face. But it was not the face of a woman, it was the face of a rough-looking man I recognised as the notorious

Cambridge Rapist, Peter Cook. He had terrorised the students of Cambridge for two years from early 1974 to late 1975, breaking into bed-sits and lodgings, wearing a leather hood and sexually assaulting the young female occupants.

Now he was on my landing at The Scrubs and had somehow managed to get himself dolled up like a tart, then persuaded other inmates to let him fellate them. In an instant, I shot the bolt on the cell door, gripped Cook by the hair and physically dragged him out of that cell, throwing him bodily back into his own. Slamming the door closed, I went and got the assistance of another officer to help me search The Cambridge Rapist's cell. What we found were pots of paint that he had taken from the art class he attended; he had used these to create a colourful pattern on one of his bed sheets, which he then fashioned into a kind of dress. In it, he looked absolutely grotesque as Cook was a small but powerfully-built man, with dark sunken eyes, a Neolithic forehead, barrel chest and long ape-like arms. I asked him what the hell he thought he was playing at and Cook told me his greatest desire was to be a woman.

There was definitely something disturbed within what passed for The Cambridge Rapist's mind. Frequently, he would appear at his cell door completely naked, masturbating; he also appeared able to attract other inmates, who may have found his notoriety fascinating. Frequently, I had to order prisoners out of his cell, as Cook got them in to suck their dicks and whatever else he could persuade them to do. Also, since I had manhandled him, he repeatedly shouted my name, saying he loved me. He really should have been sectioned, in my opinion, and I did make numerous reports about his unbalanced behaviour.

One afternoon at unlock after lunch, as I opened his door, Cook jumped out of the cell totally naked and tried to kiss me, shouting, 'Mr Sutton, I love you, Mr Sutton.'

I helped him back in as gently as I could, given the circumstances. The other staff thought this was all highly hilarious but believe me, having The Cambridge Rapist take a fancy to you was no laughing matter.

It was in late November, I recall I came home from an evening shift, feeling tired and ready for an early night. As usual, my supper was ready but I wasn't really hungry; for days, I had been ill at ease and could not quite put my finger on what the problem was. There was certainly something wrong with me, though, as just the sight of food made me feel ill. This night, I nibbled at the sausages Mary had cooked and apologised that I really couldn't eat them. Sitting opposite me at the table, Mary told me what she thought the problem was.

'I think I may be pregnant,' she whispered, 'and you are experiencing the symptoms.'

We had been married for going on six years and here it was at last, the news we had hoped for. There was a moment when we just looked at each other; I remember feeling a little faint and asked if she was sure, could we get a test, go see the doctor, etc. Mary had not, as yet, sought advice but she knew and I knew too that she really was pregnant. No wonder I had been unable to eat and was off my food; I was suffering from morning sickness. I got Mary to promise me that, the very next day, she would visit the doctor, get herself properly tested and make sure that we did everything right to ensure she and our soon-to-be baby would be safe.

We were awake till the early hours of the morning, talking about the child we had always dreamed of, how we would help this baby achieve so much, and what would they be like or become? Together, there in the middle of a prison quarters housing estate, we dreamed our dreams and held each other tight, drifting into sleep just before the dawn's first light.

CHAPTER 13

HAPPY NEW YEAR 1976

The confirmation that Mary was indeed pregnant came from our doctor in East Acton and the date expected was forecast as being the 4th of July. We had such fun telling everyone and Mary's mother was straight into the knitting; she wanted the baby to be a little girl. My grandparents in Foulridge were really delighted with this news, promising to send Mary some baby clothes. My mother had gone overseas, emigrated to Canada, so I had to inform her by letter. It was a time to plan for the future and all our friends and family were excited for us, as they knew we had been waiting a long time for this wonderful news.

The strange sickness usually associated with early pregnancy passed Mary by; it was me that had all the weird symptoms. At first, I could not even look at food; that lasted a few weeks, then I began to crave sausages. I just could not get enough of them and I could eat dozens of a certain type. Mary was calm about the whole idea of having a baby; it was me that had the worries: would we be OK, what sort of pram to buy, all manner of imaginary problems were whizzing round my mind.

On C Wing, it was fast approaching Christmas and, as I was in charge of serving the special dinner, I was determined to make a real effort. I decided that what we needed was a small choir to sing carols, happy songs to the inmates as they came to the hot-plate, so I asked around on C2 landing, if anyone would like to do this. I had, by this time, made a kind of peace with the Rastafarian inmates, who had stopped calling me 'Ras Clot', as they were getting no response and I had always treated them as reasonably as I could. So, I was really pleased when three of these inmates with long dreadlocked hair agreed to sing as a trio, in front of the Christmas tree by the hot-plate, where we were serving Christmas lunch.

I organised some practice sessions to ensure they all knew the words and were able to sing in tune. In fact, they were good and I felt certain this little choir would be a big hit with the prisoners and help to ease the stress of being away from loved ones at this sensitive time.

It was Christmas Day in the prison; the atmosphere was relatively relaxed and the staff were doing their best to make sure the inmates had as much out of cell time as was possible. I had organised the serving of breakfast, which went smoothly enough. The orderlies were enthusiastic about lunch and each had a paper party hat, to encourage a festive feeling. My trio of large dark Rastafarian choir boys were ready and in position by the big Christmas tree, awaiting my signal to start singing.

At approximately 11:45am, I advised the central office SO that we were ready to go and, soon, the first landing of inmates was unlocked. As they formed a long queue outside the hot-plate, I gave the signal for my Rastafarian choir to start singing. 'I'm Dreaming Of A White Christmas…With Every Christmas Card I Write.' Coming from the three Rasta prisoners, this caused hilarity, with inmates laughing and whistling at them. They were a big hit, dancing and singing along; everyone was having a happy experience, well, almost everyone.

I was standing by the coffee-dispensing urn; this involved one of my orderlies turning on the tap and filling the plastic pint mug of the inmate half full. This went perfectly well, until one prisoner demanded a full pint of coffee. There simply would not have been sufficient to go round all the inmates if we had poured each a pint, so I advised him that he had his ration and that was it. Unfortunately for all present, my attempt at reason was not accepted and, the next moment, this angry inmate had thrown his hot coffee into my orderly's face. There followed a battle between the orderly, trying to defend himself, and the mad prisoner, who was thumping, kicking and trying to bite the innocent orderly. In a second or so, I had gripped this bruiser, thrust his arm up his back and, with the help of another member of staff, ran him down the landing.

At the far end of C1, there were three empty cells; no furniture, just a plastic pot and a strong heavy-duty blanket. Into one of these cells we dragged the struggling inmate and, as was the customary practice, we removed all his clothing; well, actually, we ripped it off him. This inmate, though, was not accepting that he was overpowered. I could see why; he was bigger than most at around six foot, had arms like a building site hod-carrier and he was Irish. By now, the duty SO was standing in the door of the cell.

He shouted to me, 'Hold him down, let go and get out.'

That was far easier said than done, as the prisoner was still full of fight and wanted to hurt someone, most likely me, if he got chance. I decided to apply a neck hold on the man and, for a moment, cut off his air supply, a form of strangulation, in fact, that we had been taught at the Staff Training College. I was now closely physically engaged in restraining this man and he was one tough so and so, but after around a minute of applying that neck hold, he began to slow down. No wonder, really, as he could not get any air.

'Let go now and RUN!' shouted the SO at the door.

This I did, jumping up, turning quickly, and heading for the cell door, when the crazy inmate sprang up and was almost instantly on me.

'Look out!' shouted the SO.

I spun round; he was moving at a really fast rate, so the connection between his nose and my forehead was particularly fierce. The sound must have been a loud crack, though as I was delivering the 'Wigan Kiss', I heard nothing but experienced a tremendously bright flash of light as our heads met. The impact hurled him backwards and he crashed into the outer wall of the cell, where he slid slowly to the floor, completely motionless.

'My God! I've never seen anything like that before,' said the SO, as he closed the cell door.

My night duties began at 8:45pm on the Friday and I was allocated the segregation unit at the far end of A Wing. I knew my way around the place, having experienced the dubious pleasure of meeting the nameless inmate in there some months before. It was by now fairly common knowledge that the highly dangerous prisoner who had pissed on my boots was, in fact, Carlos The Jackal. He had long since left The Scrubs and, according to what we heard, Carlos had managed to escape from custody, on arrival in France.

On nights, I had no keys to open any doors, but was pleased to see the gate adjoining the Young Prisoners' unit and the Segregation Unit was open, so I could pass some time with the officer on night duty in there. Then, when I saw who the officer was, I really did smile, as I had been at the Staff Training College with this man and we knew each other quite well.

Locked up in the high-security segregation unit were many seriously dangerous and infamous killers; bombers, terrorists, sex offenders, with many serving multiple life sentences. There were also prisoners on Suicide Watch; that is, every fifteen minutes, they had to be observed to ensure that they did not kill themselves. One such prisoner was probably the most notorious child murderer in Great Britain and he exuded a sense of evil that I found deeply disturbing. It was my duty to look through the judas spy-hole in his cell door four times an hour and check he was still alive. This prisoner was extremely weird; he would sit on a chair directly behind his cell door, staring at the spy-hole with a strange darkness all about him, like a black aura. There was a distinct chill around his cell that I could discern and it sent shivers through me. I actually thought that this spooky character could hear my footsteps as I approached his cell; then he would resume his malevolent glare at the back of his door. I decided to test this theory and, on a number of occasions, crept silently to his door and looked inside, and there he was, staring hypnotically right into my eyes.

There was a mysterious connection between this murderer and myself that I never discussed with anyone at The Scrubs. Many years before, my father had been an officer with the CID, a Detective, and he had been part of the team that arrested this man. My father attended court during his trial and he told me, sometime later, that the evidence the court heard was so horrendous that grown men, seasoned police officers, wept on hearing it.

The week of nights passed without incident and I enjoyed many games of Scrabble with my colleague in the YP unit. He was a former police officer from The Metropolitan Police in London and had joined the Prison Service at the same time as me. He played a pretty mean game of Scrabble, too.

Soon, it was the 31st of December, New Year's Eve and I was spending this in the high-security segregation unit of The Scrubs. Before I left for work that night, I kissed Mary and we spent a few moments talking of our hopes and dreams for the next year, when we were to become parents. There was no doubt at all in my mind that this was to be a wonderful New Year; after all, we had waited so long for this. Mary and I shared a glass of barely alcoholic wine, drinking a toast to the future, 'To our new year and our new baby.'

It was around 11:59pm, the last few seconds of 1975, when I heard the noise commence. It was as if all the inmates on the segregation unit had started banging on their doors together. Thumping, clattering, shouting, whistling and someone had a radio on that was broadcasting the chimes of Big Ben. I was amazed at this incredible cacophony, especially as many of the inmates yelling and screaming in the New Year were serving life sentences. I listened as the final BONG! from Big Ben struck and heard, from behind one cell door, the joyous shouting of a man.

'Happy New Year!' he yelled.

On the outside of his cell, the red card showed the term of imprisonment he was currently serving; it said LIFE X 7. Happy New Year indeed, I thought, and all of it to be spent inside The Scrubs.

Back on days, I was patrolling C2 landing late one morning

just before lunch, when all the inmates were unlocked. As I walked past an open cell, I saw a prisoner seated at a table, drawing. Taking an interest, as this was something unusual, I asked the man to let me have a look. What he showed me was an amusing cartoon, depicting a group of prison officers, armed with machine guns. The subject matter was perhaps a little suspect, but this man had a talent and I asked him why he was not enrolled in the art class. He said he had previously asked but been fobbed off with some insult by another member of staff. I made a note of his name and number, then told him I would do my best to get him into the education department's art school.

There existed at The Scrubs a cultural schism between the education department staff and the discipline grade officers. It was almost as if the two were diametrically opposed in their aims and objectives. On the one hand, the jailers were seemingly determined to impose a rigid, rather draconian regime, restricting the inmates' interactions. Juxtaposed to this, the education staff, with some difficulty, were attempting to liberate their minds and encourage them to study. When I walked into the senior education officer's unit, the look on his face was one of astonishment. Discipline staff did not converse with the tutors, so I was not too surprised to sense that I was being treated with great circumspection.

When I explained why I was there, to seek help for a young man on my landing whom I believed needed their expertise, his look changed to utter incredulity. It was clear he could not believe that any Discipline Officer would make such an approach and perhaps thought it was some kind of trick. But when I explained how this man had made an effort to join the art class and been rebuffed by intransigent staff, he listened. Some weeks later, I was pleased to see the inmate cartoonist coming back into C Wing, holding a folder full of his work. He had been accepted into the art class and was making a real effort to develop the raw talent he already had.

'That's for you, Guv,' he said handing me a cartoon, showing jailers shooting up the gates of The Scrubs. The artwork had improved tremendously but the subject matter was still of a dubious nature. 'I'm going to be an illustrator when I get out,' he said and there was something in his voice that I rarely heard in a prisoner at The Scrubs; hope.

Following the Christmas period, the C Wing censors' office had a backlog of incoming mail to deal with and, on returning to duty from the night shifts, I was scheduled to work in this unit for a few days. The system was similar to that at HMP Strangeways, so I had no problem settling straight in and was quietly making progress through the many bags of mail, when I noted an incoming letter, addressed to a certain Category A inmate, located on 'C2' Landing. The envelope was of high quality and, when I opened it, I saw that the letter inside was beautifully handwritten on notepaper bearing the crest of The House of Lords. It was from a titled gentleman, who wrote in familiar terms to the Category A prisoner.

The text went along the lines of: 'Thank you so much for your letter. How delightful to hear from you and so pleased that your needs are being met by our friends there. I am doing everything possible on your behalf and will contact you again soon with good news.' It was signed 'Affectionately Yours', with a serious signature.

All Category A inmates have a special security letter file that in detail records all their outgoing mail, to whom it was sent, when it was sent and all incoming mail, when it was received and from whom it was sent. A Category A inmate may only receive incoming letters in reply to outgoing letters; no unsolicited mail is permitted. I took out the letter files for this particular Category A inmate on C2 landing and went through this with great care, but nowhere could I find a letter sent by this prisoner to the member of The House of Lords. This made me wonder how, then, could the author of the incoming letter refer, as they did, to a letter they had received: 'Thank you so much for your letter', etc.

As I pondered this conundrum, a thought came into my mind;

this particular Cat A inmate was the same one I had seen being unlocked by the Wing Governor and taken out of his cell to his office, during staff lunch break when the prison was locked down. I placed the incoming letter inside the inmate's letter file, said nothing to the senior officer in charge and made an excuse to leave the censors' unit.

I walked along C Wing and went up the steel stairway on to C2 landing, where I opened the cell of the Cat A inmate, to whom the incoming letter was addressed. I knew this man reasonably well, as I had been his landing officer now for some months and we had a working relationship. I gave the orders and he obeyed; it was always as simple as that with me. The inmates knew I would never abuse their rights and all they had to do to live a peaceful life was exactly as I told them, when I told them.

So, when I spoke to this Cat A, he was fully aware that I meant business. He was no pussy this guy, serving an 18-year stretch for Armed Robbery and closely associated with the big London gangs, but he was inside The Scrubs and there are rules in jail. I didn't pass the time of day with the man, just told him I was aware that he had been getting letters smuggled out of the prison and he was about to tell me who was doing this for him. I can still see the look of disbelief on his face as I advised him, it was tell me or he would be charged with breach of the regulations and have to face The Board of Governors.

I knew he would never want that as he was trying to get his transfer to D Wing, where his big-time criminal long-term buddies were doing cushy time. His answer was really what I had already arrived at; he told me the Wing Governor had agreed to take his letters out, when he went into his office at lunchtimes. It seemed that the Governor had made a reasonably regular habit of unlocking this Cat A and meeting with him during lunch breaks, when the jail was supposed to be on strict lock down.

'Why would he do that for you?' I asked, hardly expecting the response I received.

What he then told me was so disturbing that my mind went

into a state of high alert. This was highly dangerous and had to be dealt with immediately, as from what this Cat A was saying, the Wing Governor was seriously compromised and a threat to the security of the establishment. He told me it was the practice of the Governor to take him, unsupervised, into his office at the end of C1 landing, close and secure the door, block out the windows and engage this prisoner in sodomy.

It was, according to the Cat A, usual for the Governor to remove his trousers and underclothing, then bend over his desk while the prisoner penetrated him from the rear. In return for such services rendered, the Governor would smuggle out the Cat A's letters and provide him with whisky, cigarettes, etc. This was almost impossible to believe; it was dynamite and, if handled incorrectly, would no doubt explode in my hand. But I had the evidence and I really had to do something about it.

Having locked the Cat A back into his cell, I returned to the censors' unit and collected his letter files, along with the letter from that member of The House of Lords. I advised the senior officer of the unit that I was going to see the Wing Principal Officer. This I did and he was not exactly delighted to hear what I had to say.

'Put it in writing and take it to the CO1,' he said.

I was not looking forward to meeting that man mountain again and I felt certain he would not be best pleased to see me. It took perhaps fifteen minutes to write the statement and so, with this in my hand and a copy in my pocket, I went into the main office and knocked on the door of the Number One Chief Officer.

'Come in,' boomed his big voice and, as I walked through the door, I could see he had been expecting me as, standing beside him, was HMP Wormwood Scrubs Head of Security, a Principal Officer Mr S. Handing my statement to the CO1, I kept the Cat A letter file and the incoming letter to one side. I could see that the two men were perusing my statement carefully and both were giving me darkly suspicious glances.

'You can prove this, can you Mr Sutton?' said the Security PO.

At this point, I produced the Cat A letter file and the letter from the member of The House of Lords, which had clearly been sent in as a response to a letter that had not, according to the letter file, been sent out, in accordance with the regulations. I then gilded the lily a little by explaining that, under The Prison Act 1952 Section 41, any person who, contrary to the regulations of a prison, conveys a letter or any other thing into or out of the prison or to a prisoner…commits an offence.

For a brief moment, I thought the CO1 was going to have a heart attack; his face went from red to deep crimson and then to white, as all the colour drained away, on hearing me quoting The Prison Act to him.

'Do you think I don't know that, Sutton?' he shouted at me. 'I am the Number One Chief Officer of this prison and never, in all my thirty years' service, have I ever heard anything like this.'

He was warming to his theme now, how I as a mere Discipline Grade Prison Officer, had the temerity to question any senior rank.

'How dare you conduct enquiries into the actions of a Governor!'

I had thought about this and my conclusion was relatively simple.

'That, Sir, is my duty,' I replied.

'Get that man out of my office!' the CO1 said to the Security PO, who crossed the floor, took me by the arm and said, 'I want a word with you, Mr Sutton.'

Some days passed following my submission regarding the incident of the Cat A letter and the Wing Governor. He had not been seen since and, as I had told no one other than the Wing PO, the CO1 and his PO Head of Security, I had no way of knowing if anything was being done about my observations.

It was around 2pm one afternoon and I was patrolling C2 landing, when an inmate came up to me and said, 'What the fuck you been up to, Guv?'

I had no idea what he meant, so shrugged my shoulders and replied, 'Nothing really, why you ask?'

The prisoner, a man I knew as being no trouble, just a cell dweller, looked down to the first landing and pointed at the far end.

'You see the offices there, Guv, two senior CID in there, asking some serious questions about you'.

I was astounded; what on earth would the police want, to be asking inmates questions about me? Then another prisoner I knew quite well, the man I had helped get into art classes, came up and told me a similar story. So, I asked him what these detectives were wanting to know and it seemed they were seeking information as to whether I was smuggling letters in and out or otherwise passing illicit goods to prisoners on the landing. Of course I wasn't, but it really spooked me as, if I had been on the wrong side of any of these inmates located on my landing, here was a gift-wrapped opportunity to sail me down the river. But there was nothing I could do, nothing I could say, no way to formally complain as whoever had set this investigation in motion would say that, in accordance with their warrant held under The Prison Act 1953, they were simply doing their duty.

Nothing at all further was heard by me concerning my report about the Cat A letter and the Governor. The inmate in question was rapidly transferred from C2 to the long-term prisoners D Wing, where he was doubtless greeted by his fellow super-villains. The Wing Governor was seen only briefly following this and then transferred to another establishment. Quite what the CID Officers made of the statements from inmates on my landing, I never did discover, but a number of the prisoners came to me and said they were disgusted, as it seemed to them that the Old Bill were on a fishing expedition, trying to fit me up. Of course, I had no idea at that time that the Governor I had reported was a senior member of the Freemasons.

One inmate, a decent sort of man, really, whispered in my ear, 'They are gunning for you, Guv, watch your back'.

CHAPTER 14

ONE STEP AT A TIME

It was late January, with six months to go to our baby's arrival, and Mary was taking this pregnancy a step at a time. I was concerned, though, and attended her visits to the doctor and meetings with the nurses. BP normal, blood tests no problem, sleeping well and I know because I was there and kept on checking. I rang Mary's mother at least once every few days to give her an update; also my grandmother, Eva Walsh, in Foulridge, I kept her advised. It was an exciting time and I am sure Mary thought I was nuts, as I kept playing classical music to her belly; Rimsky Korsakov's 'Scheherazade' was my favourite, as it is so peaceful. I also talked to the not yet discernible bump-to-be and read poetry too, especially Dylan Thomas. Paul C. had given me an LP of 'Under Milk Wood', a play for words by Dylan Thomas and it had really captured my imagination. So poor Mary, who had not the first clue about who Dylan Thomas was, got hours of poetry read at her belly, as I attempted to educate our unborn child. On reflection, it seems like a mad idea but, at the time, it made sense.

On my way home from The Scrubs one Saturday afternoon, I walked into the central block, where we lived on the second floor, turned to ascend the stairs and saw, slouched across them, a number of young men. They were quite deliberately obstructing the passage and made no attempt to move as I stepped up towards them. Amongst these louts was the son of the PO I had previously spoken to, LB, and he was laid back against the stairs, slightly above the other two youths.

'If you don't mind moving, so I can get to my apartment,' I said, but I was wasting my time.

'Climb over, you silly cunt,' LB sneered.

As I went to do so, he kicked me violently, striking with his boot directly above my right eye, splitting the flesh. Blood began pouring down my face but the red I was seeing was far brighter than that. In an instant, I had the hooligan by the head and threw him against the wall, holding him tightly. The noise disturbed the occupant of a nearby apartment and the officer resident there came running out to see what the commotion was about.

'Call the police,' I said, 'this thug has just attacked me.'

There followed a momentary pause as the officer just arriving on the scene weighed up the situation. Then he went back into his apartment and dialled 999.

After approximately five minutes of waiting for the police to arrive, it was becoming increasingly difficult to hold on to LB as my damaged eye was leaking blood all over my face and had soaked my shirt. I asked the officer from the nearby apartment if he would hold this lout while I went to get Mary to look at my eye, clean and dress it. He agreed he would, so I handed LB to him, then went up to our apartment and gave Mary a shock, when she saw what a mess my eye was. She could hardly believe that the loud-mouthed gang led by LB would be so stupid as to physically assault me on my own doorstep.

'Get the police, John,' she said.

I advised they had been sent for, then came a knock at the door. The police officer came in and listened to my account of the incident, gave my injured eye a cursory glance and said, 'That is not what they are saying. They claim you attacked them.'

I thought about what had happened for a while; my right eyebrow was cut quite deeply but would heal. However, had the kick from LB hit me just an inch lower, I could have been blinded and the likely result would have been that the gang of louts would have lied their way out of any culpability whatsoever, blaming it all on me. This was quickly becoming a dangerous situation and Mary told me she was now worried, in case this bunch of thugs attacked her. Once I had changed out of uniform into my casual clothes, I told Mary to lock the front door behind me, as I went to seek an interview with the duty Police Inspector at the local police station. There had to be a solution to this nonsense; I had tried being reasonable and speaking to the parent of the ring leader, only to be shown the door.

When I finally managed to see the Police Inspector at Acton Police Station, he was not exactly helpful. It appeared that he had read the written report made by the officers that had attended the 999 call and formed the opinion that the young men were telling the truth and I had forcibly attacked them, only to be injured when they defended themselves. Despite the fact that I pointed out I lived there and they did not, despite the fact that I had sustained an injury by having been kicked in the eye, they had not a mark on them and despite the fact that this took place in the passageway to my home, he decided I was the aggressor. Not only did the police not intend to take action against LB or his gang of thugs, they warned me in no uncertain terms that, in the event of any such further incidents, I would be arrested and charged.

Looking back on this today, I can see why I was treated in this way. The Principal Officer father of LB was a Freemason and had undoubtedly contacted members of The Brotherhood in the police. At that point in time, I knew only that I was being unfairly treated. I had no idea that this was just the start of something that could cost me my liberty.

Over the next few weeks, Mary made enquiries of the neighbours in our block of apartments, concerning the activities of the bunch of hoods led by LB. What she discovered was disturbing indeed and gave me further cause for concern. One resident stated that her storage unit in the basement of the block had been broken into by this gang and they had put a mattress in there that they used for fornicating with their female camp followers. She said the unit was now full of used condoms and reeked of excrement, where they had defecated in the corner. One lady told Mary that she had parked her child's pram in the corridor outside her apartment and, when she went to use it again, found that someone, she assumed was the louts as they were hanging around, had urinated into the baby's bedding. Another mother spoke of how her nine-year-old boy had lost his push bike to these hoodlums. They not only stole his bike she said, but had pulled down her son's trousers and sexually molested him.

I myself went to see an officer resident in the opposite block that I knew from my days in the Army; we had both been NCOs in Germany, in the same regiment. He told me that this team of young bullies were frequently around his quarter, sitting on the grass with their floozies, smoking and drinking cider, then openly urinating onto the pathway. He agreed with me that this behaviour was completely out of hand but what could we do? I suggested we petition The Governor, as he was the Home Office official responsible for the good order of the prison quarters.

There are times when I have despaired of helping my fellow man and one of those times was when I approached the residents of Bromyard Avenue, with a view to petitioning The Governor for action to protect our area from the gang of louts haunting it. One really surprising conversation I had was with the serving prison officer father of the nine-year-old boy who had lost his bike and been sexually abused by the group of miscreants. When I asked what action he had taken to deal with that horrible incident, he told me he had done nothing, as he knew who was responsible and they were the sons of senior officers at The Scrubs.

'I have to think about my promotion prospects,' he said, as he declined to sign my petition.

Some residents not only declined to sign the petition, but were openly hostile. The lady that lived in the next apartment to ours screamed abuse at me as I showed her the petition, which simply asked The Governor to take action to protect occupants from the louts hanging around the quarters he was responsible for. Eventually, I managed to get about twenty signatures, which was sufficient to make a point.

The Governor patiently listened to what I had to say and accepted the petition I handed him but, he said, this was a matter for The Housing Committee and he would be passing it them for a considered response. That would be fun, I thought, handing a petition to stop the marauding hoodlums to the father of the ring leader, who was not only well aware of what was happening, but had effectively given his boy his blessing to get on with it.

Patrolling the landing on C2 one afternoon, I chanced to see my friend John C, the big Irish jailer I had first encountered slapping a hundred Young Prisoners one after the other, over a missing bun. He was walking along C1, so I gave him a shout and we went for a coffee together in what we called the wing café. John was not a happy man; he had, so he said, been given a final warning regarding his behaviour. I knew he had in the past survived a period of special probation, following his battering of the would-be escapees from HMP Brixton, so any further trans-gressions really had to be treated seriously. Over a strong black coffee, John told me what had happened.

He had been sent on Hospital Guard to Hammersmith Hospital, where the prisoner he was guarding was a patient. John had, he admitted, taken a few pints of Guinness before arriving for the night shift and, feeling sleepy, decided to take a rest. To ensure the prisoner did not escape, John handcuffed him to the metal bed-frame, then he lifted one of his pillows and slipped underneath said bed for forty winks. What then happened was that the night Sister on her rounds heard John snoring, found him under the prisoner's bed, fast asleep, and woke him up, demanding he do his duty.

John had, he said, over-reacted, as he took exception to being disturbed, and decided, if he was awake, then everyone was to be awake. So, he began marching up and down the hospital ward like a soldier, stamping his feet and making enough noise to raise the dead. This really had scared the other patients on the ward and absolutely terrorised the Nursing Sister, who telephoned the prison, threatening to call the police unless the crazy jailer they had sent was replaced immediately. I didn't like to tell John that I personally thought that perhaps the Nursing Sister had a point, as he had one of his enigmatic expressions on his face. I did cheer John up, though, by suggesting we have a sail on his boat, which was moored on the River Thames. I knew he had acquired a second-hand outboard motor and he was rebuilding it, so when it was ready, we agreed to give it a go.

One of my occasional duties as a Discipline Officer was to conduct cell searches, as nominated by the Prison Security PO. These involved me and another officer reporting to said PO at 9am and being given a list of inmates, along with their cell locations, with instructions to search them. The searches had to be conducted regularly to ensure that no contraband, weapons, or escape equipment, etc, was being stored in said inmates' cells.

On this particular day, I was handed a list of six or so cells, with names of inmates that included a number located on D Wing. I had previously experienced trouble on D Wing, with the Principal Officer ordering me off his wing. But I had my duty to do and, despite what the PO may say, I was going to do it. There is a certain protocol when visiting a wing in the prison, that is to report to the duty PO, the Principal Officer in charge, and advise him of your reason for being there.

D Wing being the long-term or lifers' unit, it operated on a slightly more relaxed regime than the others in the prison. Being aware of this, I cautiously proceeded with extreme regard to the danger of upsetting the regular staff. The PO in charge of D Wing acknowledged our arrival; I explained we had a list of cells to search, provided by the head of security, and would he be so kind as to assist us in the completion of our duties. By that, I meant tell me where the inmates were located so I could collect them and take them to their cells, which we had to search.

'No need for all that,' he said. 'Go get a coffee in our café, read the papers there and I will sign your search books when you are ready to go.'

I wondered what he meant at first and again asked him to advise me where the inmates were located, i.e. were they at work in a workshop, in an education class, or where were they? As I stood there, expecting a civil answer, I was shocked to hear this man giving me a direct order.

'This is my wing, you have already caused a near riot in the past, now I am telling you to go and have a coffee, stay in the café and I will sign your search book as completed. That is an order. Do You Understand!'

Of course, I did understand but I was not of a mind to accept that this PO had the authority to change my orders, which were to search certain cells. I considered that the Head of Security of The Scrubs had decided these cells needed searching and it was my duty to search them, so search them I would, with the help of the D Wing PO or not. When I told him this, as nicely as I could, he became extremely agitated and, for a moment, I thought he was going to grab hold of me. This was a powerfully-built man, busted-up rugby player's nose, late middle age, wide shoulders and obviously fit. He was angry, I could see that by the way his eyes widened as he glared at me.

'You cause trouble on my wing, son, and I will have you,' he growled.

Having decided to completely ignore the Principal Officer in charge of the long-term prisoners' wing, I set off with my search partner, to find the inmate at the top of the list the Security PO had given me. He wasn't in his cell but I saw that, on his red cell card, he was serving a life sentence. We found the prisoner in a Spanish language class and, when I told him to come with me as we were searching his cell, he refused. I realised that no inmate wants their property searched but there are rules in prison and I was simply carrying out my duties, so he would have to come with me. I explained this to him, but he still declined. As I gently lifted him out of his seat and twisted his arm up his back, he began shouting abuse and threats at me in a thick Irish accent.

'Youse fucking dead, youse fucking cunt,' etc.

He had a powerful voice and his insults echoed around D Wing, as I marched him along the landing to his cell. We were about halfway there, when I saw the Wing Principal Officer, along with two other officers, running down the landing towards us.

'Get your hands off that prisoner,' the PO shouted at me. 'Let him go and get off my wing immediately.'

The two officers with the PO moved as if to physically intervene, so I really had no choice but to release the inmate.

'Youse fucking had it, cunt, we knows were yah live,' the Irish prisoner said, pointing his finger at me.

'Off my wing NOW!' said the PO, pointing at the heavy iron-barred gate, leading out of the lifers' unit. This was the second time I had been thrown off D Wing for doing my duty.

In my written report concerning the incident, I noted that the D Wing Principal Officer had, from the outset, attempted to frustrate the completion of my duties. He had made it impossible for me and my partner to carry out the searches that we were instructed to do. I gave a copy of my report to the Security Principal Officer and asked him to advise me. I actually thought he would be concerned, as the searches he had deemed necessary had not been carried out, but he wasn't in the least perturbed.

'Just cross D Wing off and start on the rest,' he said, as if nothing untoward had happened.

Some weeks later, I was enjoying a rare weekend off for a change and relaxing at home with Mary watching television, when I saw on the news images of HMP Wormwood Scrubs. The breaking story was that a number of IRA prisoners were on the roof of D Wing, waving an Irish flag and making a protest. The cameras zoomed in on the roof and it was clear that the prisoners were dressed in imitation military uniforms, complete with black berets. As I looked at the inmates, around six of them, they were there, waving to the cameras and holding up the Irish flag. I was certain I recognised one of them as the prisoner whose cell I was going to search, until I was prevented from doing so by the Principal Officer in charge of the wing. No wonder he didn't want his cell searched, I thought to myself; he had obviously been hiding his uniform, ready for this rooftop protest.

The IRA rooftop protest lasted overnight and was still underway when I arrived back on duty, the following day. On arrival that morning, I was directed to join the MUFTI Squad; that is, the Minimum Use of Force Tactical Intervention team. I was kitted out with a form of crash helmet and handed a pickaxe handle, then dispatched with around twenty other officers into the roof space, directly below the tiles where the IRA protestors were standing. There was a huge hole in the roof, where the prisoners had ripped off the slates, and we could see them walking up and down, parading their flag.

The Senior Officer in charge of the MUFTI Squad ordered us to start thumping the roof with our pickaxe handles. We did this in unison, battering the tiles above us and making a hell of a racket. Then, on a signal from the SO, we stopped and someone shouted, 'Come down and we kick the shit out of you, scumbags.'

Soon, everyone was yelling abuse at the IRA prisoners and the banging on the roof started again. It was mayhem up there and I felt that what we were doing was more likely to prolong the protest than end it. The prisoners were now in fear of being seriously battered by a team of pickaxe-wielding jailers and I know they meant business; I was there. It took a long time to convince the rooftop protestors that they would not, in fact, be harmed, if they came down peacefully.

I was standing on D1 landing, still in my MUFTI outfit, when the IRA protestors came down. They had climbed up the scaffolding being used by builders to repair the interior of the unit. Now, they stood still in their mock-up military uniforms, looking weatherworn but still defiant and proud. The Governor was there, watching as they demanded to ensure that none of the MUFTI men laid a hand or pickaxe handle on them. They were lined up and ordered to remove their fake uniforms and put on regulation prison clothing.

This they all refused to do; not one of them would wear prison uniform, so having removed their handmade military kit, they stood naked in their birthday suits and that was how we marched them the five hundred yards or so across The Scrubs to the high-security unit. All the way there, inmates were standing at their cell windows, cheering and shouting at the protestors as they passed by C, B and A Wings. In a way, I felt they had proved something and made a laughing stock of the security system at The Scrubs. I believe there was a subsequent Home Office Inquiry into how this protest happened, but no one bothered to ask me. I could have enlightened them, without a shadow of doubt.

CHAPTER 15

THE INCIDENT IN THE ASKEW ARMS

My boozing buddy, Paul C, had started visiting Mary and me in our prison quarter and, on occasion, he would come for his evening meal, then all three of us would go for a drink. Not that Mary was drinking alcohol, but Paul was and I could manage a few. It was late afternoon of Saturday the first of May, Paul and I were both enjoying a Mary Special, meat pie and chips, when we heard shouting from outside.

'UNITED! UNITED!! UNITED!!!'

Looking out the window, I could see the usual suspects running up and down, waving a red shirt and yelling about Manchester United Football Club. The team had just been beaten one nil in the FA Cup and that was no doubt the reason these hooligans were making a racket. There seemed no point in saying anything to them, so we closed the windows and did our best to ignore the noise. My previous attempt to get The Governor to do something about these louts had come to nothing; no wonder, really, as the matter had been handed to the Housing Committee to deal with and that was chaired by the leading lout's father. So, the petition I had presented was effectively ignored. My complaints to the police had produced only a negative response, as they had made it quite clear they believed I was instigating the trouble.

It was around 6pm and Mary had decided to rest; the pregnancy was now evident and she opted for a hopefully quiet evening, watching TV. Paul and I did the washing up, then we set off for a few pints of beer at The Askew Arms in East Acton. It was a warm day, the sun was shining and we were in good spirits. As we walked through the housing complex, the crazy gang came running towards us, arms raised in mock Nazi salutes, yelling inanities about Manchester United. Paul knew all about the problems of the past concerning these young men.

'Say nothing, John,' he advised.

As we neared the top of Bromyard Avenue and turned left into The Vale, leading to the junction with Old Oak Road and The Askew Arms public house, I noted that we were being followed. On the other side of the road, three of the louts were keeping pace with us. I pointed this out to Paul.

'Just forget them, John,' he said.

Soon, we were in our favourite bar, enjoying a well-earned beer, after a long day's work at The Scrubs.

We were sitting at the far end of the room, some five yards or so from the entrance, when in swaggered the three amigos. The gang leader, LB, gave me a John Wayne stare, then went to the bar and started to order pints of lager. I noticed he had a cut on his forehead and blood was running down his face, dripping onto the bar top. I was just a few yards from the barman and called him over.

'You are serving underage boys,' I told him and the three young men clearly heard what I said.

They were all under the age of 18, so my observation to the landlord was correct, but perhaps not what the three vociferous United fans wanted to hear. Holding pint glasses in their hands, they moved in a menacing manner towards me.

The gang leader, LB, shouted, 'I'm gonna kill you, Sutton,' then lunged forward.

At the moment he reached out for me, glass in hand, our heads clashed and he was propelled backwards, striking the other two so hard, they all ended in a heap on the floor of the bar. LB was completely unconscious and the others were stumbling about, attempting to pull him out of the pub. The landlord appeared to be in a state of shock and Paul was standing next to me, just shaking his head in disbelief. I was just finishing my first pint of beer, when I heard the ambulance arrive, and LB was taken away on a stretcher.

It was approximately 8pm and Mary was almost in tears, as I explained what had happened. She was not at all concerned about the wannabe thug I had disposed of; she was concerned that those idiots had threatened to kill me. Now that the gang leader had failed in his misguided attempt to injure or murder me, Mary was worried that there could be more violence. We were discussing what to do next, when two police officers arrived at our door and arrested me.

At Shepherd's Bush police station, I was interviewed and, without being asked if I would like a solicitor, a statement was taken from me, in which I explained I had been threatened by three big young men, each carrying a pint glass and, when the ring leader attacked me, I had defended myself. It appeared that LB, the lout who had said he was going to kill me, had sustained a head injury and was an in-patient at Hammersmith Hospital.

He was still there some days later, when the police charged me with Assault Occasioning Actual Bodily Harm, contrary to Section 47 of The Offences Against The Person Act 1861. If convicted, the potential penalty could be five years' imprisonment. When I told Mary, she was absolutely horrified. She was seven months pregnant with our first child and I was now facing a serious charge that could possibly end up with me being imprisoned.

'What have we done to deserve this, John?' she asked. 'Why?'

At The Scrubs, I had to make a written report to The Governor, concerning the fact that I had been arrested and charged with an imprisonable offence. I half expected I would be suspended from duty pending the outcome of the forthcoming court case, but was advised that this was not to be and I had to keep The Governor updated, as the case proceeded. The next thing I needed was a lawyer so, as I was a fee-paying member of the POA, I went to see The Chairman of The Scrubs local branch, to ask for the free legal advice to which I was entitled. The Chairman listened to my request but did so in a way that made me wonder if he was as in control of his emotions as he should be. All the way through our brief meeting, he was shaking his head and twitching, eyes blinking, hands gripping the top of his desk.

In the end, he agreed that, yes, as a fee-paying member of The Prison Officers' Association, I was entitled to free legal representation and I would be immediately advised of the name of the lawyers to contact, with full details. The Chairman of The POA was, of course, the father of the young man who had been hospitalised, which perhaps explained his demeanour in dealing with me.

Victor Mishcon & Co were the legal representatives of The POA and so it was them I was advised to see for representation. This was a seriously well-respected firm of solicitors, whose practice was in Red Lion Square, London WC1. I made the call to their offices and was instructed to attend for an interview on the matter of my case; the time and date were agreed, all funded by the POA.

On the day in question, I arrived on time and was promptly seen by an incredibly bright young man, who made copious notes as I attempted to explain exactly what had happened. The fact that there was a history to this case seemed to disturb him and he asked me many times if I had intended to injure the young man, in revenge for the kick in the eye I had previously received. In the end, he decided to seek a second opinion before giving me his decision and so we went from his office in Red Lion Square, through the busy streets of central London, to other offices in High Holborn.

For a while, I waited in an oak-panelled room, all leather armchairs and oil paintings of austere-looking Judges, while the solicitor advised his colleague. Then I was called in and introduced to a gentleman, who told me he was a Barrister at Law and I must, he said, answer all his questions directly, honestly and as truthfully as I possibly could. There followed what amounted to a form of interrogation, with that Barrister virtually grilling me like a suspect. I was beginning to wonder whose side this man was on as, time after time, he asked me how this had happened, why did I not run away, was I a violent man, etc, etc.

In the end, he came from behind his desk, took me by the arm and said, 'You are not guilty and I will take your case'. There was, he cautioned, always the issue of what would happen in court on the day. 'You have to be aware that you will be speaking to a jury and they must be convinced that you are innocent.'

This Barrister was advising me that I must plead 'Not Guilty' and request that the case be referred for trial by jury at The Crown Court.

The solicitor from Victor Mishcon & Co advised me that he would send a letter giving detailed instructions and to expect this within the next seven days. I had, in the meantime, to enter a plea at The Magistrates Court of Not Guilty, following the Barrister's advice. Back home, I told Mary what the lawyers had said and she seemed more than a little relieved that my account of what had transpired was believed by those legal professionals.

The next stage was to attend court as directed and the slow legal process from plea to committal to trial by jury at the Crown Court would commence. It was some days later that I received the letter from Victor Mishcon & Co. In it, the solicitor explained that their client, The Prison Officers' Association, believed there would potentially be a conflict of interest, as my case involved one of their branch chairmen, so they were declining to act on my behalf. At first, I couldn't believe it; this was supposed to be my right to have legal representation. How could they do such a thing to me? I wondered.

There was no way I could tell Mary about this; she was now in the last few weeks of the pregnancy and already seriously stressed about my arrest. What I did do was take the letter from the solicitors and show it to as many members of staff at The Scrubs as I could and tell them just what their trade union, the POA, were doing to one of its members. The result was really dramatic, as dozens of prison officers began complaining to the Prison Officers' Association on my behalf.

I also went to see the branch Chairman myself, showed him the letter from Victor Mishcon & Co, then asked if he, acting as the head of this branch of the POA, would make representations on my behalf to the National Executive Committee. I was obviously aware that the reason the solicitors had withdrawn their services was directly connected to this man. He was, though, now in a difficult position; if he refused to act on my behalf, then it would be absolutely clear I was being treated unfairly by the trade union that was supposed to be representing me.

The word had quickly spread around The Scrubs that the POA had interfered with my legal representation and the members were disgusted. It could not have been an easy thing for the branch Chairman of the POA to do, but he agreed to contact the National Executive Committee and ask them to write to the solicitors, assuring them that there was no conflict of interest, as far as they were concerned. This they must have done because, just a few days later, Victor Mishcon & Co wrote to me again, rescinding their previous communication and advising me that they were now acting on my behalf.

My work within HMP Wormwood Scrubs continued and I had now been there for a year, so my probationary period was at an end. One afternoon in late May, my Wing Principal Officer called me in for what he told me was an Annual Report. We had experienced difficulty before, as he had told me I was trouble, following unfounded complaints made against me. But he seemed a decent man, early fifties, almost bald, with a slightly world-weary look about him, as if he had seen enough of this place.

He didn't beat about the bush, and told me that, in his opinion, my approach to duty on C Wing and in the prison generally was not acceptable. He thought I was too opinionated and had created problems. He was, he said, referring my report to The Deputy Governor, with his recommendation that I be placed on extended probation. I recall looking at the Wing PO as he said this and there was a slightly self-conscious air about him, as if he knew this was a set-up. But he did it anyway and off I went to see the Deputy Governor, who kindly advised me that my probationary period was being extended by a further six months. He also advised me that, in the event that my performance failed to improve and meet the expected standards, I would fail and my services would no longer be required.

There was, at this time, something of a problem with my sleeping; I just could not rest properly. My concerns about Mary and the baby were always in my mind and, each night, I was waking almost on the hour, to check that she was OK. When I did sleep, I experienced vivid dreams that, at times, alarmed me. One recurring dream I had concerned my late father, in which he was always walking away, beckoning me to follow him. Night after night, I would wake with that vision in my mind, of Dad motioning me to go with him. So often did this occur that I consciously decided to try.

When I told Mary, she said it was nothing more than stress, related to all the problems surrounding me and worries about our soon-to-be beautiful baby. This certain night, I told Mary, if I dreamt of my father again, I would try and see where he was directing me. Sure enough, I dreamed the same dream, in which my father walking before me made a sign with his hand that I should follow, and this I did. In the dream, my Dad entered a deep dark wood, walking along an upward winding path. I saw him clearly; he was standing at my side now, darker and darker it became as I walked, stumbling over rocks and stones. I struggled on beside him into this wood, on and up a suddenly steep narrow twisted path, with huge gnarled trees obscuring the sky and I felt weary, I felt broken.

I was crying when I opened my eyes, weeping and sobbing my heart out. Mary, hearing me, awoke and asked why the tears. I never had been an exceptionally emotional man; why, she asked, was I so upset.

'The dream, Mary. It's a hard road, Mary, it's dark, Mary, so dark.'

As Mary progressed into June with the pregnancy, I was

increasingly concerned that she may start contractions early, but she assured me the midwife was happy with everything and early July was the due date.

There was a rota operated by the Detail Office that scheduled all the duties for Discipline Officers and, somehow, I seemed to be on night shifts, every six weeks or so. I did ask to be excused night duty, pending the birth of our baby, but to no avail, so I had to get on with it. It was incredibly hot weather, with temperatures reaching into the mid-80s Fahrenheit and England in 1976 experienced the hottest summer since records began. It was even stifling hot at night and there was no way I could sleep, with Mary overheating and in some serious discomfort.

I searched all over London to try and find an electric fan, but there were none for sale; no wonder, as it was roasting. We devised a method of keeping Mary cool; I had a wet towel that I placed on her stomach and a small hand-held fan that I had wired to a large 9-volt battery. For hours, I would be awake, holding that fan on Mary and constantly changing the wet towel, to ensure she was cool. But when I was on night duty, she would be on her own.

I fashioned a support for the little fan and stood it by the side of her bed, then I ensured she had two towels, one to be draped over her stomach the other in a bowl of cold water, to be changed round every hour. This done, I kissed her goodnight and walked down the road to start a week of night shifts at The Scrubs.

The duty Principal Officer in charge of the night shifts instructed me to be the night officer in charge of the Hospital Ward. I had been there before and knew the layout but, at night, the Hospital Officer on duty was not in the main ward, but in an office downstairs. I would be there on my own. The duty did not look too difficult; I had to sit behind the ward officer's desk and maintain observations on the inmates, who were in beds all around me.

In the event of a problem, I could telephone to the duty Hospital Officer. It looked like a really cushy number and, as the night drifted by without incident, so I became more and more relaxed. In fact, I became a little too relaxed and must have fallen asleep in my chair. I was startled awake by the sudden unpleasant sensation of being kissed on the lips by a large man, who then sat on my knees.

'Kiss me…Kiss me…I love you,' he mumbled, stroking my hair.

This was a big powerful man and he was gripping me tightly in his arms, attempting to shove his tongue into my mouth. I was terrified and pushed the man away as forcibly as I could, which took some doing, as he was holding me by the head. Falling to the floor, the inmate began screaming, waking not only many of the other occupants of the ward, but also disturbing the duty Hospital Officer, who came to see what all the noise was about. I did my best to explain but the man wasn't listening, he was laughing so much.

It seemed that my passionate assailant was the infamous East End Gangster, Bernie Silver, who was on the ward, suffering from syphilitic dementia. He had been involved in a murder case and was notorious for running a large prostitution ring that had operated with virtual impunity, as Bernie Silver had been bribing the police. In fact, one of the CID Officers he had been bribing, ex-Chief Superintendent Bill Moody, was currently collecting his hardboiled 'Bent Cop' eggs in the segregation unit. That was the last time I would ever fall asleep in an open hospital ward in a prison.

On the third night of my shifts, the Principal Officer allocating duties told me I was to be put in charge of two seriously dangerous prisoners, who had that day been arrested by the Anti-Terrorist police squad. They were located in a special secure cell within the hospital complex and I was to be locked in with them. I was not exactly in their cell, which was a heavy iron-barred cage within another such cage, inside the padded cells unit of the Hospital. I was to be locked between the outer heavy iron-barred cage holding them and the other.

When I got there and they locked me in, I had a close look at my two prisoners and was amazed at what I saw. They were two rough old navvies, scruffy dirty, dishevelled and appearing to be utterly bemused.

'Wur are we, boss?' one asked and the stench of booze was intense.

I had seen on the TV news a story about two IRA gunmen who had been arrested in Brighton, armed with a WWII Army issue handgun, carrying a list of supposed victims with their addresses. One such was reported as being 'The Queen: Buckingham Palace'. That had to be a joke, as these two disorientated drunks didn't know where the hell they were. I spoke to them but got little or no sense, other than to establish that they spoke in a pronounced Irish accent and were unsure of their current whereabouts.

'Da Scrubs, now wur wud dat be?'

These two were indeed dangerous, I could see that, but the only danger they possibly presented was to themselves. I advised them to get some sleep.

It was around 2am when the singing started. 'DAISY… DAISY…GIVE ME YOUR ANSWER DO.' The racket was coming from one of the padded cells close by. 'I'M HALF CRAZY….ALL FOR THE LOVE OF YOU.' The noise was waking all the inmates up, including my two, who began yelling for help, wanting to know why they were banged up.

The Hospital Officer came along and started shouting, 'SHUT THE FUCK UP, GRAHAM.'

But Graham Young, the poisoner, was intent on singing his crazy heart out. 'ON A BICYCLE MADE FOR TWO.' Then he started again and his voice echoed round the place. The two lost souls I was caring for were complaining now, so I decided, as this was a mad house, we might as well join in. I asked the pair of dangerous gunmen if they knew the Irish song, 'Danny Boy', and as amazing as it seemed, they had never heard of it.

'OH DANNY BOY….THE PIPES, THE PIPES ARE CALLING,' I sang and saw on the faces of Butch Cassidy and The Sundance Kid a flicker of recognition; then they joined in.

'ACROSS THE HILLS AND DOWN THE MOUNTAIN SIDE'.

It was a crazy, insane singing competition, as Graham Young was really belting out 'DAISY DAISY', etc. It lasted about fifteen minutes, till the Hospital Officer returned and ordered us to stop. Then, with two strong jailers beside him, he opened Graham Young's cell and went in, holding a syringe. I heard a brief scream and the sounds of a struggle, followed by a strange silence that was broken only by the slamming of the heavy door, locking a seriously medicated Graham Young into his padded cell.

CHAPTER 16

WHAT DREAMS MAY COME

The heat of July in 1976 was intense, the hottest summer for three hundred and fifty years, and Mary was in the final days of her pregnancy with our first child. I spent hours wafting her with a big wet bath towel and we had the curtains closed to block out the endless direct sunlight. It was a late Sunday afternoon and I had washed my hair, which at the time, was quite long, dark brown and curly. Mary agreed to comb it through for me and give it a blow dry, so I slightly opened the door leading on to the balcony to get some air in and sat with my back facing that, as Mary began styling my locks.

She was standing just in front of my chair, when we heard what sounded like a tremendous wind swirling through the apartment, from the direction of the hallway inside our locked front door. There was but a split second from first hearing this unnerving sound to a powerful unseen force hitting me centre chest and knocking the hair dryer from Mary's hand. Instantly, the glass door to the balcony was blown open by the blast, so forcibly that it struck and shattered a large old earthenware pot we had positioned to hold the door open.

The whole experience was over within five seconds but it really did frighten Mary, who was certain that this was a supernatural entity. Whatever the thing was, it had thumped me hard in the chest and broken the hair dryer, as well as the antique pot. Mary and I went out onto the balcony and examined the broken remains. It had taken some force to shatter that heavy vessel. Looking across from where we stood, I could see in the near distance a church and, as I stared at this, an awful thought came into my mind. The apartment blocks that constituted the prison staff quarters on Bromyard Avenue had been built on the former graveyard of that church.

On Saturday the 10th of July 1976, Mary was six days overdue and I was really worried. When I telephoned my grandmother in Foulridge and told her, she suggested a long walk might help. Later that morning, Mary and I set off walking into Acton town centre, which was about a mile away. I bought a pack of lager and she got two big bags of groceries. On the way back home, Mary started to complain of pain but, by the time we arrived at our apartment, her contractions, she said, had stopped. I wanted to call the maternity unit at the hospital but Mary refused and insisted we wait a while. So we did, but it was really hot and uncomfortable inside our apartment.

The names we had discussed for our new child were again debated; I had suggested Jasper Cornflake if it was a boy, which was supposed to be slightly amusing but was, in fact, strangely connected to the past. I had told Mary's mum about the name and she said that, in the 1930s, there had been a free gift toy given away with Cornflakes and that was a boy doll called Jasper. She thought I had known but, of course, I hadn't. As we waited for Mary's contractions to start once more, we talked of a girl's name but could not agree, so decided to await the happy event and make our minds up then.

It was almost dark before Mary looked at me with a certain pain in her eyes and spoke quietly.

'John, it's time.'

I almost jumped off the settee, ran to the nearest telephone, located in a neighbour's flat, and called the hospital to tell them we were on our way. By this time, I was in a state of near panic, but Mary appeared perfectly calm, despite being in agony.

It was about 10pm when Mary was admitted to the maternity ward at Hammersmith Hospital and I was by her side, holding her hand; not that it helped her, but it helped me. She was taken into a private room and made as comfortable as possible in bed, as we waited for our baby. It was just on midnight when Mary's waters broke and the nurses were there helping, saying it wouldn't be long now. Mary was following their instructions and they counted the time between contractions, but nothing happened.

More time passed; it was long gone 2am and the pain became almost unbearable for Mary. She was crying out loud for help, so I ran off to get a nurse. Doctors arrived and administered medication by injection and fastened a mask to her face, connected to a supply of oxygen and some other gas, nitrous-oxide I believe, that made her become semi-conscious. Time passed; it was dawn around 6am and I was terribly worried. Why was this taking so long; Mary had been in labour for over eight hours and still she suffered. In her lucid moments, Mary pleaded with me to find out what was wrong.

'John, what's happening, John?'

No one would tell me anything; I kept asking the nurses, the doctors were constantly coming in and checking but they said nothing to me. It was almost noon and I was shaking with worry. Mary was virtually unconscious; I sat beside the bed holding her hand and said a silent prayer that everything would be OK. I had never experienced anything like this before; I did not know if this was usual but it certainly did not feel like it to me. Poor Mary lay there, eyes closed, breathing in the analgesic gas, gripping my hand as the pain spasms caused her to wake momentarily. Time passed, more doctors arrived and I knew that this couldn't be right. It was almost 4pm now and I saw that the nurses appeared nervous.

It was around 6pm on Sunday 11th July 1976 and Mary had been in labour for over twenty hours. She was brave and so strong, but I could see she was really suffering now. I was feeling useless, helpless and about to demand answers, when one of the doctors came up to Mary's bedside and motioned for me to follow him.

'We are sending for a senior consultant,' he said. 'There are complications with the birth.'

That was it, complications with the birth of our baby; what kind of complications, what about Mary? The room was again empty, save for Mary and me; her breathing was shallow and I sensed she was slipping away. Where were the nurses, where was that damn doctor? I sat by her bed, holding Mary's hand talking to her, quietly saying it would be OK and that I was there. Yes, I was there but there was nothing I could do and that distressed me, seeing my Mary suffering.

At approximately 7:45pm, a team of doctors and nurses came into the room and wheeled Mary out into an operating theatre. I went to follow, got as far as the door, saw a surgeon all masked up and a team by his side, then they led me away; I was not allowed in. For one terrifying minute outside that door, I heard Mary screaming, then someone shouted, 'Do It!'

Fear ran though me. Faith must have faith that all will be well. I kept saying to myself: Mary will be OK, our baby will be OK, this is just a complication, all will be well. I had absolutely no idea about the procedure in a maternity unit; we had been told to expect a short time of Mary being in labour, then, as the contractions came closer together, she would give birth. Mary was just twenty-nine years of age, she was healthy, a strong fit woman and determined. She would be OK, Mary would be OK, our baby would be OK. On and on I said this, walking up and down, up and down the corridor.

It seemed like hours, and I was trembling. Mary will be OK! At approximately 8pm, the consultant surgeon came out of the theatre; he removed his mask and spoke to me. At first, I couldn't quite grasp what he was trying to explain; what he said made no sense. He mentioned something about the birth being unusually difficult, a syndrome, a series of problems. Was Mary OK? I asked. He said she was sedated but I could not see her, nor could I see the child. I was crying now; why? Why could I not see Mary and what was wrong with our baby? I had seen lots of films where the parents are together shortly after the birth of their child, looking happy and smiling together; why not Mary and me? What had happened? They wouldn't tell me.

'We are doing all we can,' he said, then turned and walked back into the theatre.

A nurse came and I was taken away to a private room, then given a cup of tea, which I could barely touch. There was utter confusion in my mind now; something had gone wrong and they were hiding it from me. I was starting to fear the worst. After perhaps half an hour, a doctor came in to speak to me and I could see by the way he was looking that this was bad news. What he said almost broke my heart; it seemed that our baby had been born with what he described as potentially life-threatening physiological abnormalities. The baby was alive and being examined by a consultant paediatrician. Once this examination was complete, I would be advised.

'Will our baby live?' I asked.

The doctor just looked at me. There were so many questions but there were no answers. The feeling was almost indescribable; it felt like I had been kicked in the heart and, within me, was the most awful heavy ache. The doctor excused himself, then called for a nurse, who led me away to a hospital ward, where I saw Mary, completely comatose in a bed. She looked weary, washed out, pale and drained. For an hour or so, I sat holding her hand but she didn't know; she was asleep, deeply painlessly, mercifully asleep.

The long walk back to our apartment was just a blur. I had been almost forty-eight hours without sleep and was numbed by the stress, as all manner of terrible thoughts went through my mind. In the apartment, I found Snowy, Mary's pet, was in need of a walk; how I managed that, I will never know. Then I started on the lager we had bought together on that Saturday afternoon, a lifetime ago, and I drank tin after tin after tin, till I collapsed on the settee.

What dreams came to me; these were not dreams, these were nightmares, as I lived over and over again the awful hours I had shared with Mary, as she screamed in pain. The savage sunlight woke me, blazing through the windows, shining straight into my eyes like an interrogator's searchlight, burning brightly into my brain. Somewhere in Hammersmith Hospital, my wife, Mary, and our new-born daughter we had not yet seen, waited for me. I was a dishevelled, stinking wreck, having slept in my drink-soaked clothing. All around me were empty beer cans and a half full tin of baked beans, spilled across the carpet. How the room had become such a mess I did not know, but I felt sick.

The clock on the wall said 6:30am. I was due on duty at 7am but there was no possible way I could work. All I could think of was getting back to Mary and finding out just what the problems were with our baby. She needed me now, immediately, and I sensed she would be waking alone in a strange bed, no baby, and I had to get to her.

I ran the bath full of cold water, took off my shoes and climbed in, fully clothed. The shampoo lid must have snapped as I emptied the bottle over my hair; the entire contents poured out. Soon, there were soaking wet clothes, soggy socks, water and bubbles all over the bathroom. I towelled myself dry, got a complete kit change and was out of the apartment by 6:45am.

At just after 7am, I was in Hammersmith Hospital at Mary's bedside and she was just waking. At the foot of her bed was a cot and, within that cot, lay a beautiful little baby, without covers. I saw a name on the front; it said 'SUTTON'. This was our baby and she looked to be turning blue.

I shouted at Mary, 'Why is the baby not covered?'

A nurse came to me.

'What's wrong? Why is our baby going blue?'

I was angry now; I was crying and sobbing, wondering why they had left our baby without covers and why was she going blue? Was she dying?

'WHY!' I yelled at the nurse and, suddenly, we were surrounded by staff.

A Ward Sister took me by the arm, and a doctor came to me. Mary was still half-doped; she had no idea what was happening.

'Dear God! Tell me what you are doing to my baby,' I shouted at the doctor.

More staff arrived; the nurses stared at me in a really strange way, as if they knew something. Then I knew, too, but I could not accuse them. A fierce anger burned within me; this was my baby, this was our baby, and she had to live.

Within two minutes of me entering the ward, our daughter was taken away to an intensive care unit and placed inside an oxygen life support system. I was finally allowed into the ICU and saw her there, wired up with a saline drip and heart monitor, looking so frail and tiny. I could not touch her; the nearest I got was a yard or so away, but I could see she was living.

'Come on, little girl, you can do it,' I said, as the tears flowed.

This was our baby, the child Mary and I had dreamed about all these years and she was going to make it, she was going to live. Inside me, there was a terrible thudding ache in my heart; how could this be, poor little baby and Mary, Mary, my poor Mary.

Back in the ward at Mary's bedside, I found her almost awake, though still bemused as to what was happening, as no one had been able to tell her anything, due to the sedation. Now she was compos mentis again, we needed to talk and it was really about time for some answers.

'What has happened, John?' Mary asked, sitting up in bed, holding my hand.

I told her about the Intensive Care Unit and that our baby was alive, being cared for. Neither of us knew what the real problem was, so I went to seek out the Ward Sister and ask her what this was all about. I was aware that the consultant had told me there were physiological difficulties with the baby but there was nothing specific. The Sister agreed to get a doctor to come and speak to us, so I sat by my wife's bedside and we waited.

'Dulcie is her name,' Mary said; we had talked about many names and, yes, I liked that.

'Jane. Dulcie Jane,' I suggested and so it was agreed that our little baby girl would be called Dulcie Jane Sutton.

'Does she look like a Dulcie?' Mary asked, as she had yet to see her baby girl.

The doctor arrived, a middle-aged gentleman, professional demeanour, slight smile and an understanding manner. What he then told us was difficult, difficult to accept. He said that our baby had been born with a rare and serious genetic defect that was potentially life-threatening. The syndrome was extremely uncommon, with only one hundred and fifty such births world-wide per year. No doctor in Hammersmith Hospital had ever seen a case like this before and there were many vastly experienced paediatricians working here. He explained that the survival rate for such live births was less than 40%, due to severe heart, lung and thoracic abnormalities.

Babies with such multiple infirmities were, he said, usually stillborn, due to the long and always painful labour. Our child had so far beaten the odds and was doing well in the ICU, from where he had just come. Mary looked in shock, though I saw something in her eyes, as if she knew this was not the whole story we were being told.

'What is it, Doctor?' she said, tears rolling down her cheeks.

He looked at me for a moment and his smile had vanished.

'The syndrome is extremely complex and you will both be seen by our most senior paediatrician, at the earliest opportunity. I can tell you that the medical name given to this is The Ellis-Van Creveld Syndrome. Among the many physiological abnormalities, there is the incidence of polydactyl and chondroectodermal dysplasia. Your child has an extra digit on each hand; she is of short stature and there are further complications that will be explained to you by our senior paediatrician.'

I looked at Mary and held her hand.

'Dear God help her,' I said, shaking with emotion.

As the doctor walked quietly away from Mary's bedside, I sat there, looking into her eyes. We were both completely lost with this; how could it be, why did it happen to us? One hundred and fifty births with this syndrome worldwide and we were in that number; the odds must have been millions to one against.

'She's a pretty baby,' I said, holding Mary's hand. 'Let's go see her, let's say hello to our little Dulcie Jane.'

There was a wheelchair at the side of Mary's bed and she had been told not to walk, so I wheeled her down the long corridors of Hammersmith Hospital to the ICU. The nursing staff recognised me and allowed us in to the foot of the enclosed unit, within which lay our tiny baby girl. We could just see her little face, eyes closed and mouth slightly open. There followed a moment, as we just stood staring at our little miracle.

'She looks like you, John,' Mary said and I could see, in a way, Dulcie Jane did have a look of me, which was hardly surprising, as I was her father. 'On top of her other problems,' Mary joked and, in that instant, I knew we would get through this together and our beautiful little baby would survive.

Mary stayed in the maternity ward at Hammersmith Hospital for ten more days, visiting Dulcie at the ICU. It was a difficult period, as even the doctors were uncertain of any definite prognosis, so rare was the diagnosis. However, as each day passed, Dulcie Jane grew stronger and began to gain weight. Then, one brilliant morning in mid-July, the consultant paediatrician allowed our baby out of the ICU and on to the ward with Mary. From there, it took just a further two days before we were allowed to bring our baby home.

When we arrived back at the apartment and Mary saw the mess I had made of it, she was absolutely furious. There were empty beer cans scattered everywhere, half-eaten bags of fish and chips, I had trodden a cheese sandwich into the carpet and squashed pieces of half-eaten toast on the settee. The bathroom was a filthy mess, with soaking wet towels and a bath full of mucky water. In the kitchen, I had emptied all the cupboards, broken the electric can opener, spilled baked beans into the sink and something was definitely rotten in there. How this had happened, I did not know; my mind had been in utter confusion since the birth of our baby.

'You lazy, bone-idle bastard,' Mary cried and it took her five straight hours to put the place back in order.

Later that day, when the apartment was cleaned up, we sat together and enjoyed a few quiet moments. It was an incredible feeling, that first time to be with Mary, holding our child, Dulcie Jane. After a terribly traumatic experience, we were at last as one, in the place that for now we called home. I can remember nursing our baby, just holding her in my arms; Dulcie seemed so small and delicate. Then, when she opened her tiny eyes and looked at me, I could sense within those sparkling blue orbs a glimmer of determination. The words of a long forgotten poem came into my mind: 'Tyger, Tyger burning bright, in the forests of the night…. In what distant deeps or skies, burnt the fire of thine eyes.'

CHAPTER 17

THE SWEENEY

I was soon back on duty at The Scrubs, patrolling C Wing, making a living as a Prison Officer. On my landing, there was a celebrity inmate, whose name and image had been all over the media; on TV, front pages of the press, with banner headlines stating: 'GEORGE DAVIS IS INNOCENT'. Supporters of this convicted prisoner had even dug up the Test Cricket pitch at Headingly in Yorkshire. Roger Daltry, the lead singer of pop super-group 'THE WHO', had appeared on stage wearing a T-Shirt supporting the 'FREE GEORGE DAVIS' campaign. Davis was claiming that the CID in London had 'fitted him up'; that is, according to him, the police had fabricated a case against him and planted evidence.

I spoke with George Davis and he was a larger-than-life character, full of stories about his East End gangster friends, such as The Richardsons and The Krays. He told me that the case in question, the armed robbery of the London Electricity Board offices at Ilford on 4th April 1974, was nothing to do with him. He claimed the police had planted evidence, some samples of his blood they had previously taken, to secure a conviction. Davis was, he said, well and truly fitted up by certain CID Officers, who were determined to have him imprisoned. When I asked him why, he laughed and told me that the police knew he was 'bang at it', doing robberies all round London but couldn't prove anything so they had, said George Davis, 'stitched him up'. Davis was popular with his fellow inmates and I could see why so many were supporting him; he was funny, interesting and gregarious, as well as being a seriously connected villain.

There was a letter waiting for me when I arrived home from my duties at The Scrubs, one day in late July. The letter was from my solicitor, stating that I had to attend before the Magistrates, to be formally committed to trial at Crown Court. The wheels of the legal system were turning and soon I would have to stand trial. When I told Mary, she just shook her head, smiled and handed me baby Dulcie.

'Twinkle, Twinkle Little Star, How I Wonder What You Are.' I sang her a nursery rhyme.

This baby needed her father and there was no way I was not going to be there for her. No way could the court find me guilty; John Sutton Is Innocent. But no pop superstar was wearing a T-Shirt with my name on, there was no campaign to protest that I was being fitted up. All I had was Mary and my Dulcie Jane, yet I knew that would, in some way, be enough.

Directly outside the main gates of HM Prison Wormwood Scrubs, there was a large red brick building that served as a hostel, a half-way house between prison and release. This hostel provided long-term inmates with a chance to integrate back into society, by residing there and working in the community, immediately prior to release. There were approximately fifteen occupants within this unit and, as part of the rules of residence, they had to be inside the doors by 11pm each night. There was a night duty officer in charge of the hostel and his duties included booking all inmates in and reporting to the duty Principal Officer within the main prison.

One Saturday night, the duty officer in charge of the prison hostel was me. I had never undertaken this post before but had no reason to consider that this was going to be a troublesome task, as all the inmates were on their way out of jail soon, so they would not want any trouble. I got my sociology books and was looking forward to a quiet evening, with a good opportunity to revise for the forthcoming written examination. The first year of my London University Diploma in Sociology examination was just days away and here was a great chance to read up on the subject, to prepare myself.

By 10pm, the hostel was virtually full, with all the occupants booked in, except one. I did a quick check of the premises and counted all present and correct, other than the single missing inmate. There was still an hour to the regulation deadline, so I was not at all concerned, just aware that one more inmate had to check in before I could report my numbers to the duty P.O. I was reading a book on The Social History of Great Britain, dealing with the National General Strike of May 1926, a matter that was close to my heart, as my paternal great-grandfather, Thomas Blacklock, had been the leader of the North West Miners in that strike.

It was soon 11pm and no sign of the missing hostel inmate. My numbers had not yet been called in to the duty PO and they were now due. I decided to give the prisoner ten more minutes before reporting him absent. My judgement proved right as he staggered in through the hostel's front door at precisely 11:10pm. As I had just made a pot of tea, I advised him to take seat in the kitchen next to mine and have some hot tea to sober himself up, as he was clearly under the influence of alcohol. I clearly recall he wanted two sugars and plenty of milk.

Having telephoned in my numbers as all present and cor-rect, I made an entry in the hostel log that said the inmate had arrived late by ten minutes. I showed the man what I had done but advised him that, as no one ever read the damn thing, there would be nothing further said. That seemed to cheer him up and he wanted more tea and a talk. It sounded like a lot of nonsense to me, what he was saying, but he told his tale with great enthusiasm and seemed to be enjoying himself.

He was saying something about what a great day he had enjoyed in London and what a brilliant success it had been. One thing he did say that stuck in my mind concerned an incident that, at the time, I assumed was from his past, as he had been an armed robber and was at the end of a nine-year sentence.

'We got them into the back of the shop, tied them all up and helped ourselves,' he said, sniggering and chuckling to himself.

'More tea?' I suggested and poured cup number three for him, spooning in the two large sugars.

On the Sunday morning, following my night duty in charge of the hostel, I walked home along Du Cane Road and stopped at a newsagent's, to buy a Sunday newspaper. I was casually looking at the front-page headlines when one caught my eye. It was The Sunday Mirror and, in bold black letters, it read: 'Armed Robbery At Jean Junction'. I bought a copy and, as I slowly walked home, I read the salient details on the front page.

'We were taken into the back of the shop, where they tied us up,' said the shop manager.

The account of what had happened during the armed robbery at the retail outlet Jean Junction, 81 Kings Road Chelsea, was almost word for word what the drunken inmate at the prison hostel had told me. When I arrived home, I sat down and read through the headline story again and noted that, at the end of this, it said: 'Anyone with any information should contact West End Central CID' and it gave a telephone number.

There was no doubt in my mind about the information I had. That inmate had been drunk, yes, but his detail was too exact to be fantasy and, at 11pm on Saturday night, the papers had not gone to press, so he could not have read about it. I knew full well that, as a prison officer, my duty was to report what I had heard to the Principal Security Officer at HMP Wormwood Scrubs. That was what I was supposed to do; however, having experienced the utter ineptitude of that PO, I had absolutely no faith that he would take any effective action whatsoever. I knew it was at least partly his fault that the IRA had been able to dress themselves in mock military uniforms and make a laughing stock of the jail, by parading around on the roof of 'D' Wing. So I decided to ignore my instructions to report everything through the correct channels at the prison and I went to telephone West End Central CID, from the public payphone on Bromyard Avenue.

The officer who answered my call at the police station in central London listened as I told him what I had heard, where I had heard it and when. He then asked me to repeat what I had said, which I did. I gave my name and my address, then he told me to go home and someone would be calling round to see me. I had Snowy, Mary's dog, with me so we took a slow stroll back to the apartment, calling at a few trees on the way.

It was approximately 9:30am when two CID officers knocked on our door. Mary answered and invited them in. I was asked to tell them exactly what I had seen and heard, which I did, giving as many details as I could recall. At 9:45am, I was in an unmarked police car, being driven to a police station in Ealing. Once there, I was taken to an interview room and a smartly-dressed man in his late thirties introduced himself to me as Chief Inspector 'M' and said he was from The Serious Crime Squad.

I knew a bit about that unit; they were colloquially known as 'The Sweeney'. He sat down with me and meticulously asked me to start at the beginning and tell him everything I knew about the incident and how I came about this information. At approximately 10:15am, the Chief Inspector took me to a telephone and instructed me to call the Governor of HMP Wormwood Scrubs and advise him that The Serious Crime Squad were going to search the hostel, as they believed it was being used as a base for armed robberies. I did try to tell the Chief Inspector that the Governor would not be best pleased with this and he advised that, in such case, I should hand the telephone to him.

It took at least ten minutes to get the security unit at HMP Wormwood Scrubs to connect me to the Governor, who was doing his daily rounds. When I told him that he was speaking to Officer Sutton and I was in Ealing Police Station with a Chief Inspector of the Serious Crime Squad, he point blank refused to believe me. Handing the telephone to said Chief Inspector, I listened as he tried to explain to the number one Governor of The Scrubs that, in the opinion of the Serious Crime Squad, his hostel was being used to house a gang of armed robbers, who were using it as their base from which to operate.

The end result was that the Governor agreed to check out the

Chief Inspector's credentials and call back to Ealing Police Station. It took almost thirty minutes for a call to come through and it was from the Principal Security Officer of HMP Wormwood Scrubs, who said he would meet the Serious Crime Squad at the hostel immediately.

The Sweeney consisted of six CID Officers, all carrying hand guns, which they checked before we ran out of Ealing Police station, jumped into two unmarked fast cars, switched the sirens on and raced through the streets to The Scrubs. When we arrived, the Security PO was standing by the front entrance to the hostel, looking rather perturbed. The head of The Sweeney introduced himself and asked the PO to show him in.

'I'm afraid you won't be allowed to search the hostel today,' he said. 'The inmates are not there and Home Office regulations state that, during any search of an inmate's property, they must be present.'

I could see this wasn't what the Chief Inspector wanted to hear and he wasted no time in telling the PO what he thought about his response.

'Get The FUCK out of my way or I will arrest you for obstructing the police.'

The PO looked shocked.

'John, show my men the way in.'

Well, I had no key to open the door and I was not about to ask the PO, so I just took a run at it and booted the damn thing, shattering the lock, and it flew open. I ran in, followed by six armed officers of The Sweeney. The place was deserted there was not a single inmate there. I checked the log book and saw that, between 10:45am (shortly after I spoke to the Governor) and 11am, every single resident had signed out. This was hard to believe; Sunday morning and all the inmates had signed out within a fifteen-minute period! The Governor and his Security PO had clearly ordered that the hostel be evacuated.

The Chief Inspector asked me to help his men open the inmates' private lockers; I just kicked the doors in, smashing them one at a time. The place looked like a bomb had hit it when I finished stamping all the locked cupboards and wardrobes into pieces. After almost an hour, the head of The Sweeney took me to one side and told me what they had found. It seemed that the newspaper reports had not contained all the known details. The armed robbers at Jean Junction had used fake police warrant cards to fool the manager and his staff into going quietly to the rear of the premises, where they were subsequently tied up. During the search of the hostel today, a number of these imitation warrant cards had been found, along with a fake police uniform. I was then taken back to Ealing Police Station, where I had to write a lengthy and detailed statement. It was almost 3pm by the time I arrived home.

The police, I was advised, were now searching for the missing inmate, wanted in connection with the armed robbery at Jean Junction. There was a police officer detailed to await his return to the hostel but, of course, he never did come back. Some days later, the Chief Inspector of The Serious Crime Squad attended HMP Wormwood Scrubs and asked to see me.

'Have you thought of joining the police, John? I will get you straight into my team,' he said.

I am sure he would have done so, had it been at all possible for me to join but I could never be a policeman like my father had been and my brother was. I am almost completely colour blind, so could never pass the medical examination. The Chief Inspector thanked me for being so attentive and contacting them; I would be receiving a police commendation, he said, on his recommendation. That though never did happen, what I did get was a formal caution from the Number One Governor concerning my conduct; I had breached standard operational procedure by contacting the police directly. It was, the Governor explained, my duty to report anything unusual to the Principal Security Officer or the Number One Chief Officer. I felt like telling him what I thought of those two clowns, but I suspected he already knew. The formal admonishment was added to my record of service and I was now effectively on a final warning.

I was patrolling C Wing, when I saw my best boozing buddy, Paul C, walking towards me and he looked really happy. We went together into the wing café and, over coffee, he told me the good news. His wife had given birth to a baby girl; mother and daughter were doing fantastic, he said, and he had come to say farewell. There would be no time for us to go out and celebrate, Paul said, as he was leaving for Liverpool by train that evening. The Home Office had granted him a compassionate transfer and he was due to report at HMP Liverpool, also known as Walton Jail, at 7am the following Monday.

I was, of course, delighted for Paul; he had been trying to get back to his wife for over a year and had finally done it. As we shook hands, Paul assured me that, when it came time for my trial at Crown Court, he would be there to give evidence for me. He had already supplied my solicitor with a statement and it simply said what he had seen and my legal advice was that this man was a good witness for the defence. I thanked Paul for his assurances and we promised to keep in contact but, as he turned and walked away, closing the big iron gates of C Wing behind him, I felt really sad.

Paul had been my friend, a crazy fall-about drunken intellectual poet and a pal. I thought of the time he had been on parade, covered in pig shit, how we had thrown the Chinese restaurant hijackers into the street, how we had watched the brilliant Alan Badel playing Richard III, how we had listened to 'Under Milk Wood' by Dylan Thomas and how he lost his ability to speak when pissed. I remembered how his sweaty socks had nearly got him expelled from his lodgings; then I heard the iron gate slam shut behind him and another chapter in my life came to a close.

CHAPTER 18

NO WAY, MINISTER

On my landing C2, there were a number of inmates from the Traveller community, serving long prison terms for violent offences. These were really rough, tough, bare-knuckle-fighting hard men, who had mercilessly injured their adversaries. We got along well and I found them to be humorous, easy-going people, who just wanted to do their time peacefully, or else. No one on the landing was in any doubt that these Travellers were best left alone.

I liked them a lot and offered to help, if they would accept. None of them could read; they were all virtually illiterate. I asked, did they want me to try and teach them; much to my surprise, they agreed to try. The prison education department allowed me to borrow some basic literacy books, gave me some plain paper and a few pencils. Over the next few weeks, I started a daily routine with these men; I would show them a picture in one of the books with a word underneath, an apple image with APPLE underneath, and so on. They were to help each other and, at the end of each day, just before lock-up, I would test them. In return for my help with this, they agreed to teach me their Traveller language, Romany.

Things were going really rather well with this project and my students were making progress. I had even managed to get them to start copying the words they were learning onto the sheets of paper. For my part, I had mastered a few Romany phrases. Get behind your door: Chevvy an ya jigger. The boss man is coming: Fester gellen mudder rag. I was pleased with the way things were going till, one day at lock-up, the eldest of the Travellers said they were not doing it any more. I asked why, as they were doing so well.

'Me brain hurts,' was the answer and they all looked serious about this.

I thanked them for trying and promised to help again, if they changed their minds. I felt really sorry for those men; not only were they locked inside a prison, they were also locked out of society by their illiteracy.

According to my scheduled shifts, I should have been on a rest day, but there was a staff shortage at The Scrubs so everyone was automatically called in on their rest days. The only way to get time off was to go into the main office and request this in writing, handing the application to the Principal Officer and, even then, it was not guaranteed that you would be granted it. This was, in my opinion, a form of abuse and I was not at all amused to be told that, at The Scrubs, it was normal practice to work thirteen days out of every fourteen.

Most of the staff I spoke to about this seemed pleased to be working all the hours that God sent, as the overtime was at an enhanced rate, with double time at weekends. There were staff who had worked thirty consecutive days, 7am to 9pm. They had a name for these characters; they called them 'Overtime Bandits'. On this working rest day, I was detailed to take charge of a prisoner in Hammersmith Hospital, who had suffered a minor heart attack. This kind of duty was considered by staff to be something of a cushy number, as all one had to do was ensure that the prisoner in the hospital bed did not abscond. I had done a number of these Hospital Guard duties and usually took the opportunity to catch up on my reading for the Sociology Diploma course I was studying.

When I arrived on the ward at Hammersmith Hospital, the officer I relieved reported to me that the prisoner had experienced a quiet, incident-free night. There was a problem, though, he said; the prisoner was former Cabinet Minister and member of The Privy Council, Mr John Stonehouse. I was not too concerned who it was, really, but I asked the officer why he thought this was problematical.

'He still thinks he's in charge,' the officer said, 'so good luck with that.'

There had been rumours in the jail that Stonehouse was pulling a few strings to get his own way. I had been hearing about his chess games with a certain Governor, so he had managed to arrange preferential treatment. Also, John Stonehouse had demanded the workshop radio be tuned in to BBC Radio 3, the classical music station, as he objected to pop music being played. I could see a slightly amused look on my colleague's face, as he turned to leave me in charge of this potentially difficult inmate.

The prisoner was just waking from his sleep and I recognised him as the former Postmaster General, John Stonehouse. His face had been all over the news on TV and in the press, following his faked death by drowning in Miami, Florida USA, where he had left his clothing on a beach. The reason being that he had fraudulently transferred all the funds from the private bank he owned into his own accounts elsewhere, stealing hundreds of thousands of pounds. He had subsequently done a disappearing act and was caught almost by accident in Australia, when police searching for Lord Lucan stopped Stonehouse by mistake.

So, I knew quite a bit about this prisoner and his history as a high-flying politician. All that, though, made no difference to me; I was there to ensure he remained in custody and that was that. I took a seat at the side of his bed and began reading the book I had brought with me, 'Captain Swing' by Eric Hobsbawm and George Rude.

Stonehouse did not say anything at all to me, as he received his medication followed by the serving of breakfast. In fact, I noted that he was deliberately doing his best to ignore the fact that I was there. The nursing staff appeared attentive; more so than usual, I thought, and he was all condescending supercilious smiles.

It would have been around 10am, when Stonehouse turned

to me and, in a certain tone that I must admit carried a natural authority, said 'Officer, could you collect my copy of The Times and get me a bottle of Lucozade from the canteen?'

I had to hand it to him; this guy actually thought he was addressing his own personal assistant and did so in a manner that almost made one want to do his bidding, almost. Politely, I corrected the mistake Stonehouse had made, explaining as gently as I could that he was, in fact, a prisoner and I was his jailer, not his fetch-me-carry-me slave so, no, I would not be collecting his copy of The Times or bringing him a bottle of Lucozade. There followed what may be described in a romantic novel as a rather strained atmospheric silence. Stonehouse quite clearly had been accustomed to giving orders to the prison officers guarding him and expected them to be obeyed. I could see he wasn't happy about my refusal to wait on him and I observed a definite flicker of disapproval, as I had reminded him of his current status as my prisoner.

I was reading about the agricultural workers' uprising in the 1830s, following the invention of threshing machines that made many land workers unemployed, when I saw Stonehouse motioning to the Ward Sister. She came over to the opposite side of his bed and I faintly heard him making a complaint that I had declined to collect his newspaper, etc. The ward Sister appeared disturbed by what Stonehouse had said to her and she almost marched round to my side of his bed, put her hands on her hips and gave me a short lecture about how all the other prison officers had gone to the canteen for John Stonehouse and it was my duty to do the same.

Now, I knew precisely what my duty was, in respect of the prisoner in the hospital bed; my duty was to ensure that he did not escape from lawful custody. This I carefully explained to the Ward Sister and, to better help her understand, I showed her my Warrant Card and advised that, in the event that she attempted to obstruct me in the commission of my duties, I would arrest her. This was, I succinctly advised, a Home Office production to hospital and the prisoner was in my charge, not in the charge of the hospital.

I gently pointed out that she should immediately get about her duties and cease at once from interfering in mine, as to do so constituted a criminal offence. For all I knew, she could be a party to some devious cunning plot to spring Stonehouse from jail, by distracting his custodian. Whatever her reason was for inappropriately approaching me, she now had her answer. The look of shocked surprise on the Ward Sister's face was something to behold; she stood there fuming, thunderstruck; if I had slapped her with a wet fish, she could not have appeared more startled. I suspected that no one had spoken to this woman in such a direct way for a long time; obviously, she wasn't getting out enough.

Stonehouse, who was listening to this insidious exchange, pulled a petulant sulky face, then turned over in his bed and looked the other way. Ignoring the glowering nurse, I picked up the copy of 'Captain Swing' and returned to my sociological studies. It was around 11am, when an officer I knew from The Scrubs walked onto the ward and approached me.

'You've been ordered back to the jail, I'm your replacement,' he said and I could see, at the far end of the ward, the Sister was glaring at me.

Back in The Scrubs, I reported to the detail office and was advised that the CO1 wanted to see me. We had met a few times before and I was not so far impressed with the way he performed his duties. Inside his office, I was treated to a loud and bombastic lecture on how we at HMP Wormwood Scrubs had to maintain a good working relationship with the nursing staff of Hammersmith Hospital and how I had just jeopardised this by upsetting the Ward Sister. By this time, the CO1 was really getting on my nerves; his apparent lack of understanding of the regulations concerned me, so when he had finished telling me what a cunt he thought I was, I told him exactly what the law stated. This was becoming really tedious and I suspected I was wasting my time but he needed to know he was wrong.

'The Prison Act 1952 Para 13 Section 2 states: 'a prisoner is in legal custody when outside a prison but under control of an officer of the prison'.' I then asked the CO1 if, in his opinion, in the case of John Stonehouse on the hospital ward, who was the officer of the prison; was it me or was it the Ward Sister?

'Get out Mr Sutton,' he grunted. I was beginning to doubt the sanity of this man.

My maternal grandmother, Eva Walsh, had appeared completely unannounced at our door, one Saturday afternoon. Mary was out shopping, pushing Dulcie in her pram; on returning, she discovered Grandma sitting on her suitcase, waiting. It was a brave thing for Grandma to have done, as her home in Foulridge, Lancashire, was at least two hundred and thirty miles away and she had travelled all that way by bus.

'I've come to see my little Princess,' she said.

I recall my grandmother was so happy, holding Dulcie Jane, singing to her and just giving our special baby so much love and affection.

'Nothing wrong with this child,' she said and, for two weeks, Grandma never left the apartment, just spent all her time cuddling and talking to Dulcie.

My grandmother was seventy-one years of age at the time and suffering from an incurable form of cancer, but she would not let that stop her; she was determined to see our beautiful baby. Just watching her bathing Dulcie Jane, holding her close, singing nursery rhymes quietly to the child till she slept, brought tears to my eyes. This was our baby; she was a wonderful child, a gift from God and, to my lovely old Grandma, she was a little princess.

I had always been close to my grandmother and grandfather; they used to take me on holiday with them to Blackpool when I was a boy. Now I had a baby, her first great-grandchild, my grandmother was there to help as best she could and it meant so much to both Mary and me. There was, though, some upsetting news she had to tell me, concerning the house on Cromwell Street, which I had bought from her and Granddad. The agreement had been that the house be transferred into my name and I pay what amounted to about 25% of my earnings to them by standing order each month; this I had been doing for over a year. The house had a sitting tenant and I was happy to leave everything as it was in that respect, with my grandparents using any rent to maintain the property.

This had all been going really well and the house deeds had been put in my name, with the money I paid making a big difference to the lives of my grandparents, who were both on the Old Age Pension. Grandma explained that my mother had been complaining that the property I had bought from them was rightfully hers. I didn't want to distress my grandparents, as the whole idea was to help them and help Mary and me in the longer term. Whatever my Grandma wanted me to do regarding this, I would do.

The answer was, I should instruct the solicitors to make a deed of gift to my mother, transferring ownership of the house from me to her. Poor Grandma; she didn't want to have to ask this of me, as she must have known I had struggled to pay the money each month. I simply said not to worry and to forget what had been paid; it was only money. Then I assured my grandmother that it would be done.

When I told Mary, she just smiled and shook her head. 'What next, John?' she said, 'What next?'

The time came for the legal proceedings against me to be progressed to the next stage. At Acton Magistrates, I attended for committal to Crown Court. A representative from the solicitors, Victor Mishcon & Co, attended to represent me and, in the dock, I was asked to make a formal plea.

'Not Guilty.'

The solicitor stood up on my behalf and requested that this matter be set down for trial by jury. The magistrates confirmed that the case would be submitted to Knightsbridge Crown Court, with a specific request that it be heard at the earliest opportunity, due to the nature of my employment. I was remanded on unrestricted bail, to attend Knightsbridge Crown Court on a date to be set.

The solicitor from Victor Mishcon & Co advised me that, as I had opted for trial by jury at Crown Court, there would be no further financial support for legal fees from either my trade union, The POA, or the Legal Aid system, as I was not eligible. I was advised that a note of the charges already incurred and details of the fees for further representation would be forwarded to me immediately by post. I asked somewhat apprehensively if they could give me an estimate of what I might be expected to pay.

Without so much as an ironic smile, the lawyer replied, 'The Barrister you have already instructed will be charging at £1,000 a day, the solicitor at £500 plus costs and I consider this to be a two or even a three-day trial, so expect the account to be in the region of three to five thousand pounds.'

I didn't dare tell this City of London solicitor that I hadn't got a pot to piss in and that what he was suggesting amounted to the totality of my annual wages, working as a jailer at The Scrubs. This was one piece of information that I simply could not burden my dear wife, Mary, with. I had to carry this crock of crap all on my own.

CHAPTER 19

KNIGHTSBRIDGE CROWN COURT

Dulcie Jane was christened at Leigh Parish Church on Sunday the 3rd of October 1976. This was where Mary and I had been married, six years before. It was a real family get-together and, following the ceremony, we all went back to Mary's parents' house on The Avenue in Leigh and shared a light buffet they had prepared.

It was while I was standing in the rear garden of the house that I began to feel a strange sense of unease. Living next door to Mary's mother and father was her uncle, a rather curmudgeonly old rascal, who had previously insulted me. As I stood looking at the rear of these two adjoining semi-detached houses, I saw something dark creeping across the brickwork from the uncle's house towards Mary's parents' back door. I thought this was a shadow, but it was mid-afternoon and daylight.

As I looked, the darkness continued to creep, slithering sideways and finally disappearing into the house. A chill tingling shiver ran through me as I saw this and a silent voice in my mind said, 'Something wicked this way comes'.

Within a split second of hearing that mysterious disembodied voice, I saw, opening the wooden gate between the two adjoining properties, the man Mary called her uncle. He was in his late seventies, slightly stooped over, silver-grey hair, small of stature but smartly dressed in an old-fashioned worsted suit. Beside him was a small rather rotund middle-aged lady, perhaps forty years of age, dressed all in shimmering black and she was fussing around the elderly uncle, as if he were a little boy. There was an unearthly chill in the air and absolute unnatural silence, as I stood transfixed, staring as they walked towards the back door of the house, entering together.

It took me a few moments to regain my composure then, as calmly as I could, I went back indoors, to rejoin the christening party. Mary was there, with Dulcie in her arms, chatting to her sister, Susan. I looked around and saw the elderly uncle helping himself to the pork pies, but nowhere could I see the lady in black. The whole affair lasted no more than an hour or so and, soon, everyone had wished Dulcie Jane well, then gone home.

Now, there were just Mary's parents, the baby and us. Something was troubling me, though; I had heard that silent voice, seen the eerie crawling darkness and where had that woman in black gone to? Over a cup of tea in the back room, I asked Mary if she had seen a middle-aged lady dressed all in black with her uncle. No, she had not, she said, but asked me if I thought I could recognise her, which I knew I could, as she had passed just a few yards from me on her way into the house.

'Is that her?' Mary said, pointing to an old framed photograph on the wall above the fireplace.

I stood up, walked over and looked closely; the photo was of a lady, aged around forty years, wearing a black Victorian-style dress, standing beside a pram, in which there was a pretty little baby. Next to her was a neatly-dressed boy of around eleven years.

'Most certainly, that is her, no doubt about it,' I said.

Mary's mother Alice spoke next. 'That's Mary Thomas, my mother, the little boy is my brother; as you know, he lives next door.'

There was a second or so of silence as what she had said registered in my mind. I asked if this lady in life had always been over-attentive to her son and Mary's mother laughed at that.

'Definitely. Forever fussing around him; he was her spoilt little treasure, a precious boy,' she exclaimed.

I looked again at that old sepia-toned photograph and an odd uneasy sensation ran through me. There was something disturbing about the way the little boy was looking at the baby, sitting in the pram by his mother's side. I could see on his face a dark malevolent grimace that, to me, seemed pure evil.

'Who is the baby?' I asked Mary's mother.

She smiled. 'It's me,' she said. 'That was taken on the day I was christened.'

They were long days for Prison Officers at The Scrubs; you had to be on the wings, ready to go at 7am, Monday to Friday, 7:45am Saturday/Sunday and, perhaps twice a week, there would be a late shift, ending at 9pm. You often had to work thirteen days out of fourteen. The pay, as a basic rate, was not sufficient to allow anything more than mere survival, so all the staff worked overtime. The average total hours worked per week by a discipline officer were in the region of sixty. Some staff worked all the hours they could get, but sacrificed their social life completely.

I tried to avoid overtime as best I could, but the POA at The Scrubs had agreed a compulsory overtime regime with management, so there was no way out. The really weird thing was that the trade union; that is, The Prison Officers' Association, had on its HMP Wormwood Scrubs branch committee, a chairman who was also the Principal Officer in charge of the staff detail rota. Other committee members were also in senior positions of authority in the jail, so any representations to the POA made by a relatively junior officer, such as me, were made to the people you were complaining about.

I recall trying to get my late shifts changed, so I could attend the London University Sociology Diploma course I was taking and being told to sort out an exchange myself. Weekends off were subject to the requirements of the detail rota and there was simply no way to opt out, at least not according to the POA.

My friend, the rather eccentric giant Irishman John C, found himself in further trouble, having attempted to repair his boat's outboard motor inside his single officer's accommodation. I was in the prison club on a Sunday lunchtime, quietly completing a crossword and sipping a lemonade shandy, when John C ambled in, looking agitated. He came and sat with me, then offered to buy me a Guinness, but I couldn't accept as I was on duty. He really just wanted someone to talk to.

John had, he said, been fixing an outboard motor in his one-bed officer's flat and, to test it, filled the bath with water and propped it up, with the rotor blade submerged. When he had started it, the power had been so great that he lost control of the motor and it had shattered the bath. John looked more than a little concerned and, no wonder; when I asked him how he had managed to stop the motor, he shook his head and said, 'It's still going. I ran out and shut the door.'

Something had to be done so I agreed to go with John and have a look at the damage and, if needs be, we would together find a way to halt this thing. His prison accommodation was just along Du Cane Road, a few yards down from the prison; we were there in a minute or so. He opened the door of his flat and I could hear a faint rumbling sound, which we followed, entering the bathroom where, to our astonishment, we saw why the noise was so faint. The motor had chomped and chewed its way through the wall adjoining the next flat and was now somewhere inside that accommodation. There was a huge hole in the wall; bits of brick, plasterboard, paint and the remnants of his bath were scattered all around and the place was dripping wet through.

'Only one thing to do,' he said. Guiding me back out of his flat, closing the door behind him, he headed straight back to the bar and ordered a Guinness.

Victor Mishcon & Co wrote to me with details of their charges and the current account was already approaching one thousand pounds. The good news was that they had managed to secure an early date at Knightsbridge Crown Court for my case and it would be heard in late November. I spoke with Mary about this and we both agreed it would be a weight off our shoulders to get it out of the way. The constant worry was like living with the sword of Damocles hanging over my head. There really could be no peace of mind, while the threat of imprisonment was waiting around the next corner. Not that I had any serious doubts about the outcome; I was quite certain that I was not guilty and had acted in self-defence, but as the Barrister had said, it depended on the day and the jury.

That evening, I telephoned Paul C in Liverpool and advised him of the forthcoming trial date; he agreed he would attend and speak in my defence. That was somewhat reassuring, as Paul had been standing next to me when I was attacked and had seen exactly what happened.

One Saturday morning, when I was enjoying a day away from The Scrubs, Mary suggested we go for a stroll into London and have a look at the street market on Portobello Road. It was early morning and, having enjoyed one of Mary's bacon and egg breakfasts, I was ready for some fresh air. Mary had been asking me for some time if we could visit the open-air market at Portobello Road, so we put baby Dulcie in her pram and set off walking. It was a little less than three miles and we were taking our time, just strolling along, happy to be out in the sunlight.

In the hectic days leading up to and including the birth of our baby, I had missed Mary's birthday, so I thought now was a good time to buy her a present. The market at Portobello Road had hundreds of stalls, selling all kinds of antiques and collectibles. There really was something for everyone; old fur coats, military uniforms, brass candlesticks, stacks of 78rpm records, boxes of costume jewellery, old postcards. You name it, this market had it. I felt certain I would find here an ideal birthday present for my wife.

We were standing at what I would call a junk stall, all odd ornaments, tins full of buttons and stacks of bric-a-brac. Mary was in her element, rooting through the stuff and I stood holding the pram, quietly content to let her enjoy herself.

'This is an old soul.'

I looked up to see an elderly lady, wearing an old-fashioned jet-black hat with a dark feather at the side. She was standing at the front of Dulcie Jane's pram. I watched as she stooped forward, peering in at her little face, just peeking out from the pink covers.

'She has been here many times before,' the lady said, staring intently at our baby girl.

I was intrigued by these comments and, in a friendly manner, asked how she knew such things.

'You know too, don't you?' She smiled, reaching to touch Dulcie's cheek. 'I see the gift in your eyes.'

This fascinated me and, when Mary returned to my side, I went to introduce her to the mysterious lady, but suddenly she wasn't there. I looked all around but she was nowhere to be seen; it was, I thought, an incredibly strange encounter.

It was now my turn to have a search round the stalls for that special birthday present for Mary. I wanted something different, a unique gift that she could treasure forever, reminding her of our day at this magnificent market. She agreed to wait for me, taking a seat by the iron railings, while I went for a walk round the stalls on Portobello Road . It took me just a few minutes to find what I was looking for and, after a moment's haggling, I got the stallholder to agree a price I thought realistic. They even put my purchase in a big plastic carrier bag, having wrapped it up in tissue paper. I was delighted with this and felt certain that Mary would love it. I have been wrong before when buying Mary things but not this time; I just knew it was an absolutely ideal gift.

Back at the pram, I handed it to her: 'Happy Birthday, Mary….Happy Birthday To You,' I sang and watched in hopeful expectation as she removed the paper and examined her present.

'A stuffed ostrich!' she shouted, causing people to look round. 'What the hell am I supposed to do with that?'

I could see she didn't like it. (As I write this book, it is 39 years since that day and Mary still has her stuffed baby ostrich so, in a way, I was right. But at the time, she was angry with me.)

On C Wing one morning, I was detailed to act as an instructor to a newly appointed prison officer, who was in the first week of his induction period. It did not seem so long since I had been in that position myself, so I knew what information he would need. The man was in his mid-forties and ex-military; he had, in fact, been a Warrant Officer in the Royal Air Force. He seemed frightfully keen to learn everything there was to learn about C Wing and how it functioned. The man had a little notepad and wrote everything down. He examined all the documents, the cell cards, landing incident books, Category A lists, the whole lot. It was as if he were conducting more of an inspection than just familiarising himself with the way it all worked.

I tried to lighten the intensity a little by introducing him to the 'Paraffin Lamps', but he was not amused, made some notes, then gave me a strange stare. I took him for a coffee in the C Wing café and tried to get him talking about his life. His first name was Charles and he had been, he explained, the most senior Warrant Officer in the RAF, holding that rank at a number of prestigious establishments. Charles had, he said, met Her Majesty the Queen on numerous occasions, when he was in charge of military parades.

This man was just way too serious for my liking; he quite obviously enjoyed being in uniform and was out to impress. Then he told me that the Home Office had agreed to provide him immediately with accommodation for his wife and family at HMP Wormwood Scrubs. This was, as far as I knew, unheard of, so he must have been specially recruited and put on the fast-track promotion scheme. I knew that such programmes did exist, as Vicious Vic, the training PO at Strangeways Jail, had told me he had removed my name from the scheme.

Over the next few weeks, I saw Charles going about his duties and spoke to him a few times, asking how he was enjoying life as a jailer at The Scrubs. He was always polite, if a little aloof, and told me his regular posting was in D Wing, the long-term inmates' unit. I was aware of what that place was like and advised him to watch his back and keep his eyes open as, in my opinion, the senior staff were over-friendly with the prisoners. I recall that my advice was not well received by Charles, who quickly terminated our conversation and walked off.

Some weeks later, I was in the prison club, passing my lunch hour chatting to an officer I knew, who worked on 'D' Wing, and asked him how Charles was doing.

'What do you know about this?' he asked, in a suddenly severe manner.

Of course, I actually knew nothing but the thought came in my mind to ask about the fast-tracked ex-Warrant Officer, who had impressed me as being a little too keen.

'He's been required to resign,' the officer told me.

It seemed that, almost as soon as Charles had joined the staff on 'D' Wing, he had been targeted by the long-term, highly experienced inmates. They had 'befriended' him, made him feel like one of the boys, gave him praise for being such a 'good screw' and persuaded Charles that they would ensure he was a brilliant success in his new important position. Then these highly sophisti-cated inmates had cajoled poor gullible Charles into running bets for them to the local Bookmaker's Betting Shop. Once he had done this a few times, Charles was blackmailed into smuggling in booze and tobacco.

However, as he was a complete amateur at what is officially termed 'trafficking', he had been observed by staff buying packets of rolling tobacco in the prison club, when they knew he did not smoke. Coming into the prison one afternoon from his lunch break, Charles had been stopped and searched; secreted on his person were bottles of Whiskey and packs of tobacco.

He could have been prosecuted under The Prison Act 1952 but, instead, no doubt to save the Home Office embarrassment, he had been required to resign. I had tried to caution the man that D Wing was not exactly what it appeared to be and that all within had to be treated with great circumspection. Charles, though, had known better, or so he obviously thought; now he was on another fast track, out of his prison quarters and into harsh reality.

Knightsbridge Crown Court was a rather austere building that gave me a distinct sense of unease as I entered. Mary was with me and she seemed quietly confident that I would succeed in proving my innocence. I was certain in my own mind that all I had done was to defend myself, but the police didn't agree; they had charged me with Assault Occasioning Actual Bodily Harm, contrary to Section 47 of The Offences Against The Person Act 1861. If found guilty, I could possibly be sentenced to a period of up to five years' imprisonment, so this was a really serious matter indeed. I looked around the reception area and was relieved to see my Barrister, who took me to one side and quickly explained the proceedings.

I had to present myself to the court ushers and surrender my bail, then be escorted to the court, where I would enter the dock. A jury would be sworn in and the trial would commence, with the Barrister for the prosecution opening, then calling witnesses. Mary was by my side, listening to all this; my poor wife, she gave me a wistful smile, then wished me good luck. She stood silently watching as the black-suited court usher led me away to the dock, where I was to stand trial as the accused.

Having confirmed my name and formally entered a plea of 'Not Guilty', the case for the prosecution began. The first witness was the young man, LB, who had made the complaint to the police and he told the court his version of events; how, according to him, he had just crossed the floor of the public house to have a word with me, then I had struck him a blow that knocked him unconscious. Medical details were given about his admission to hospital and how he had been concussed, with a suspected fractured skull. Then came his cross-examination by my Barrister, during which the man was asked if he had at any previous time entered into conflict with the accused.

'Well, I kicked the cunt a few times,' was his rather uncouth reply, which was no doubt duly noted by the jury.

The next witness was the landlord of The Askew Arms, who had been present, serving behind the bar during the incident. He basically stated that, as I spoke to him about serving people under age, the young man had crossed the room, approaching me with two others immediately behind him. He did not, he said, see exactly how the man was struck, but saw him fall backwards, knocking over the other two so that they all fell to the floor, where the man remained totally unconscious. Under cross-examination, the landlord stated that, as he was serving the young man, he noticed that blood was dripping from his forehead onto the bar and that this was before the incident.

The two other young men, who had been with the injured party, were individually examined in the witness box; both said that, though they did not see what struck their friend in the head, it was so powerful that it had propelled him backwards and knocked them over. My Barrister then asked how their friend had sustained the wound to his head that caused him to drip blood on the bar as he was ordering beer.

Their answer was, 'He was in a fight outside the pub before we went in.'

I was the first witness for the defence and explained to the court that I had been in The Askew Arms, quietly enjoying a beer with my colleague Paul, after a long day working in HMP Wormwood Scrubs. I saw the three young men walk up to the bar and recognised them as being the louts who caused trouble in the housing complex where I lived with my wife. I knew that the leader of this group was under the age of eighteen years and, as he was ordering beer in a public bar, was doing so unlawfully. I had called the landlord over and advised him of this fact.

The next moment, I heard the young man I knew as LB shout, 'I'm gonna kill you, Sutton,' and saw him with his two friends, quickly crossing the room, holding a glass in his hand.

I knew that behind me was a solid brick wall; there was no way out, as to my right was the bar and to my left a series of tables and chairs. With no available escape route, I had a split-second to decide upon how to protect myself from this six foot plus man, who was approaching me in a menacing manner, having stated he intended to kill me.

As he came close and lunged at me, there had been an unfor-tunate clash of heads and he had fallen backwards, colliding with his two friends. The cross-examination was somewhat unnerving, as the Barrister for the prosecution suggested that I was a former boxing champion and therefore an expert at self-defence. I had to agree, yes, I had been a middleweight boxing champion in The Army and I was highly trained in the art of self-defence, which would enable me to defend myself against an assault, which was exactly what I had done.

Paul C was the only other witness for the defence and he explained that he was standing immediately behind me, with his beer on the bar top. He had seen the three young men cross the room, heard one shout a threat to kill and, the very next instant, they were all in a pile on the floor. Paul said that, although he was there, he could not say exactly how this had happened, as it was so quick.

When asked by the Barrister for the prosecution if he thought I had head-butted the young man, Paul simply said that, if I had done so, then he did not see it. Once Paul had given his evidence, the Judge called a halt to the proceedings and ordered that the trial would recommence at 10am the next day. That night, Mary, who had been observing the proceedings in the public gallery, said she was confident I would be found not guilty.

'He came across as a big thug,' she said, referring to LB and his statement about kicking me.

The following morning at 10am, I was standing in the dock at Knightsbridge Crown Court, waiting for the proceedings to commence, when I noticed two rather burly men, seated in the public gallery. I had not seen them there the day before and wondered why they were in court. The dock officer was a jailer from HMP Wandsworth and he seemed an affable kind of man, so I asked him if he knew who the two big guys were.

'They are your escort to prison,' he said.

It seemed that a report on the trial had been passed to the authorities and a decision had been made that it looked as if I would be found guilty and sentenced to imprisonment, so these two jailers were there to take me straight to a nominated Category

D Prison. Mary was there, too, sitting just behind the two officers waiting to take me away; she looked quietly composed.

The Barrister for the prosecution summed up by telling the jury that I was a dangerous, bad-tempered man, who was an accomplished expert in both boxing and martial arts. The young man had, he said, only wanted to speak to me and, when he came up to me, I hit him so hard that he had been instantly rendered unconscious, causing him actual bodily harm.

My defence Barrister explained that I had done nothing more than defend myself against a much taller man and his two accomplices, who had approached me armed with beer glasses, having first threatened to kill me. My Barrister also pointed out that the injury complained of by LB could not, without reasonable doubt, be as a result of his encounter with me. The complainant had, according to witnesses for the prosecution, been injured in a fight outside The Askew Arms before he came in and, when he did come in, he was already bleeding from a wound to his head.

The Judge summed up, gave the jury their directions and, by noon of the second day, they were sent out to consider their verdict.

My Barrister, his assistant, Mary and I were seated in the canteen of the court, having a cup of tea while we awaited the verdict. Mary was reassuring me that all would be well, as she said one of the members of the jury had smiled at her. I felt that the case was obvious; I had acted in self-defence and, had I not done so, I could quite possibly have been badly cut, had the young men managed to hit me with the glasses they were carrying.

The Barrister said he was confident, but a jury is a unique entity and one can never be certain till the foreman delivers the verdict. That really did cheer me up. I had barely had more than three sips of my tea when the sound system announced that the jury in my case were back in court. It had been no more than ten minutes and this seemed to me unusually rapid. Mary took my hand as we walked back into court but we could not speak; it was so stressful.

The Judge looked around the court and, for a moment, stared directly at me in the dock; then he turned to the jury.

'Have you reached your verdict?' he said.

I was looking straight ahead; whatever happened next, I had to live with this.

'How do you find the defendant, Guilty or Not Guilty?' he asked and, for a moment, I must admit I felt a little afraid.

If guilty was the verdict, then I would likely be off to some prison cell, but I wasn't guilty, I knew that.

The foreman of the jury stood up, a middle-aged man, neatly dressed and with a clear deep voice, he said, 'Not Guilty.'

The moment was like someone had lifted a massive weight from my shoulders. I looked across at Mary and she was smiling with relief. The Judge dismissed me from the dock and I was a free man again. It felt good; in fact, it felt brilliant.

Outside the court, I used a public telephone to call HMP Wormwood Scrubs and advise The Governor of the outcome of the court case. The switchboard put me through and I was connected to his deputy, who sounded astounded when I told him that the verdict was not guilty.

'Not guilty?' he said. 'Are you sure?'

As if I would be inventing something like that. I then asked him to transfer my call back to the switchboard; without saying another word, he did. I then had my call redirected to the Detail Office, where I advised Principal Officer B that I would be reporting for duty in the morning, as the verdict was not guilty. I waited for a response but heard only the ominous sound of silence, then the line went dead.

As it did so, a quiet voice in my mind spoke to me. 'This is not over yet, John.'

CHAPTER 20

I RECOGNISE THAT TIE

One morning, as I was escorting a group of inmates back to C Wing from legal visits, I saw John C. He was doing the rounds of the jail with a team of prisoners, collecting rubbish and shit parcels. I could see John was looking a little distressed; his shirt was undone and he just appeared unkempt and dishevelled. There was definitely something amiss and I spoke to him briefly as we passed, arranging to see him in the prison club during lunchtime.

At 12:30, we sat together in the bar; John had his Guinness and I had a ginger beer. He told me the bad news; following the damage to his single officer's flat and a further complaint from an inmate, The Governor had called John in and demanded his resignation. He had no choice but to put this in writing and would be leaving The Scrubs forever at the end of the week.

'How will I get a job now?' he asked. 'Where will I live?'

He was a fine big fellow, my friend John C, and it didn't seem right that he be forced out of his position for a few mistakes. Though I could see why The Governor would have to do this as, no matter how much I enjoyed this man's company, he was something of a danger to work with. Then I had an idea. I knew the officer who was in charge of the cleaning party that emptied all the bins in the main office; it was John C. I told John that what he had to do was get me a sheet of headed notepaper from the stack of stationary on the secretary's desk and I would write him a letter of reference. He had to go in there to empty the bins with his team of prisoners. All he had to do then was take that letter to Ireland and apply to The Irish Prison Service and he would, I assured him, get a job, no problem.

Of course, I knew that The Civil Service, of which The Home Office was a part, never gave individual references. However, what John needed now was a confidence booster, to give him hope when all seemed lost. His eyes shone with delight at the idea and I quickly took notes about his service, to include in the script. That done and after another two pints of Guinness, he set off back into the jail, to complete his duties with the dustbins and attend to his mission. We agreed to meet outside the jail at 5:30pm and John would have the notepaper for me.

At home, I had my father's old typewriter that I was been using to write my essays for the Diploma in Sociology. I slipped the formal headed notepaper, bearing the Home Office Crest and address of HMP Wormwood Scrubs, into the machine and set about fabricating John C a brilliant reference.

'To Whom It May Concern. It is with great regret that I have accepted the resignation of Prison Officer John C, who has served within this establishment with great distinction for a number of years. John C has been an established Prison Officer since 1965, serving at HMP Brixton before transferring to HMP Wormwood Scrubs in 1975. I have absolutely no hesitation in recommending this man as an honest, trustworthy and dedicated employee. Yours faithfully, Mr H. Governor.'

Then, using a fountain pen and black ink, I forged the signature. When I handed it to John C the next day, he was absolutely delighted and said he would be using that to apply for a job in Dublin. That was the last time I ever saw John C, though I did hear about him some years later from a member of the Northern Ireland Prison Service. They said John was now a Prison Officer at Mountjoy Jail in the Republic of Ireland and was infamous all over Dublin. I was so pleased to learn that my friend had done well.

HMP Wormwood Scrubs was at full capacity and a decision had been taken to transfer a number of Category B prisoners to HMP Winchester, some 70 miles away to the south. There were four inmates and four staff, along with a driver in a large dark blue

HMP Van. The inmates were handcuffed together in pairs and it seemed like a nice easy day's duty, just riding along in the back. I knew the other officers, as we were all regular staff on C Wing; the man in charge of the escort party was a hulking great Scottish officer, called Mr McB.

There was something of the showman about McB; he was a man who liked to hear his own voice and he had lost the volume control. When McB shouted, the whole jail heard what he had to say. The journey to Winchester took us from 8am to almost noon, as the traffic was heavy. On arrival at the jail, we were advised that the transfer could not take place until 2pm, as the reception unit staff were not present. Our prisoners were located in a holding cell and we were advised to take an extended lunch break, then report back at 2pm. We did not need telling twice and, within five minutes, all four of us were ordering food and drinks in The County Arms, a nearby public bar.

We were happily enjoying our meat pies with a pint of best bitter, swapping sinister stories of dark exploits inside HM Prisons, when our Mr McB jumped to his feet, put his uniform hat on, adjusted his jacket, stamped to attention and, like a military guardsman, he marched across the room. Standing at the bar was a respectable middle-aged gentleman, reasonably smartly dressed in a suit, looking quite relaxed, enjoying a glass of beer, while thumbing through a copy of The Racing Pink.

Up to him strode all six foot four inches of the mighty McB, who smartly halted, snapped his heels together, threw up an elaborate salute and boomed out for all the bar to hear, 'Regimental Sergeant Major McB, at your service, SIR! I recognise that tie!'

There followed a short rather uncomfortable silence, as the obviously startled gentleman tried to take in what this uniformed giant standing stiffly to attention before him had said.

I could see the look of utter incredulity on his face as he stared McB in the eyes and said, 'Why don't you just FUCK OFF!'

It was hilarious; there was this 20 stone hulking great uniformed balloon, with a half-stoned gormless look on his face, standing like an oversized toy soldier, having the piss ripped out of him by a little guy, dressed like a bookmaker's clerk. We did laugh at that. McB was, in fact, a member of the Junior Territorial Army for children and he held the honorary rank of Sergeant Major. All the way back to the jail, we were shouting, 'I recognise that tie,' till I saw that Mr McB had reached boiling point; his head was steaming.

By 2:30pm, we had processed the prisoners and handed them over to the reception staff at HMP Winchester. We were just about to exit the jail, when I saw a man I recognised as one of the senior medical staff from The Scrubs. He saw me and came over, asking if it was possible to get a lift back to the prison in our van. McB was either half-pissed or sulking, so assuming command, I said sure, why not, and invited him to jump in the back with the rest of us. He was an amusing companion and told us some strange stories of his life as a doctor in The Army, before joining The Prison Service as a General Medical Practitioner. We dropped him off about a hundred yards before The Scrubs on Du Cane Road; he didn't want anyone seeing him in the van, he said, swearing us all to secrecy, as he was, no doubt, claiming expenses for the journey.

The walk from HMP Wormwood Scrubs, after a long day's work, back to our apartment on Bromyard Avenue included an underpass that took you beneath the busy main road. I always used this route, as it shortened the journey and seemed perfectly safe to me. On one particular evening, I had been working a late shift, ending at almost 9pm, and it was completely dark as I made my way down Du Cane Road to the pathway leading to the underpass. I was wearing a civilian overcoat on top of my uniform and, at a casual glance, I would have looked, I suppose, like any other member of the general public. Without really thinking about it, I walked into the darkness of the underpass and was perhaps half way in, some fifty yards or so, when I saw a man shining a torch and talking into what looked like a two-way radio.

He was saying something like, 'Will do, message received. Roger, over and out.'

He was wearing a prison officer's uniform hat and had a military-style jacket on, giving him the appearance of a police officer. As I passed him, I took a close look and saw that this was, in fact, a member of the staff at The Scrubs. I had seen him many times on duty on B Wing, the Borstal Allocation Unit, where my buddy Paul had worked. I knew him as Mr G.

'How you doing, mate?' I said and, as I spoke, saw that in his right hand, he was holding a packet of Embassy Cigarettes, not a two-way radio. For a second, he obviously did not recognise me and mumbled something about being on duty. This struck me as extremely weird indeed and, as I walked away, I wondered to myself what the hell he was really up to.

It was some days later that I was patrolling C2 landing, when an alarm bell rang; this was to call all available staff to the central control office on C1 landing. I ran down the metal stairs and was immediately directed to get myself to B Wing, where there was an incident. The distance was about two hundred yards or so and took me no more than thirty seconds, as other staff had already opened the iron gates. Once inside B Wing, I reported, along with half a dozen of my fellow staff, to the central office there.

The Senior Officer in charge told us that there was a hostage situation and we were to be prepared for action. We followed the SO to the far end of B Wing and, there, he pointed to a door that led into the external cleaning party store room. In there were kept the big brushes, bins and shovels, used by the cleaners to keep the exterior of B Wing clean and tidy.

'He's got three Borstal Boys in there,' the SO said.

We did not understand this; 'he' had Borstal Boys as hostages in the store room? Who was this, we wondered. It seemed that the prison officer in charge of the cleaning party had locked himself into this storeroom and was holding three members of his team, young Borstal Boys, hostage. What we had to do was get them out of there safely.

The SO was trying to hold a conversation through the door with the officer, but was getting no sense at all. The boys he had in there could be heard shouting for help and it was decided that we would take the door off its hinges, by use of a powerful hydraulic jack. The Works Department arrived with the equipment and, within a few minutes, the door was forced and we dragged it away, allowing access to the storeroom. I immediately recognised the officer in there; he was Mr G, the weirdo who had been talking to a packet of cigarettes in the underpass, a few nights before.

The Borstal Boys were all half-dressed; one was stripped to the waist. Mr G was in disarray; his shirt hanging out of his trousers, which were wide open. He was holding one of the boys by the arm. With madness in his eyes he glared at us.

'Get back!' he screamed.

There was a sudden rush, as the two free Borstal Boys ran out of the storeroom, which gave us plenty space to get in. Without hesitation, I physically rammed Mr G backwards, a solid left fist centre chest propelling him rapidly to the rear, gently bouncing his head off the brick wall. Two other members of staff gripped the officer by the arms and dragged him from the storeroom. It was all over within a few seconds and the Borstal Boys were out, seemingly uninjured.

We handed Mr G over to the SO and his B Wing staff, then returned to our duties on C Wing. I later heard that the three boys were alleging he had been sexually interfering with them in the storeroom. As far as I know, no one at The Scrubs ever saw the man again and I was told he had been admitted to a psychiatric unit.

Mary, with our little daughter Dulcie Jane, was slowly settling into our apartment on the Bromyard Avenue complex and, though it was not where we wanted to live, it was for the time being home. My studies at the Ealing College continued, as I had passed the first-year examinations of the London University Diploma in Sociology. I was really proud of that and, to me, it was something of an achievement. Also, I loved the reading and the essays I had to submit were enjoyable, as I was using my ability to write, which I had always wanted to do.

For a few weeks, it seemed as if we were going to be OK with my work in The Prison Service. We had put all that nonsense with the louts behind us and I was determined to make a go of this job. I had to earn a living and now we had a baby, there was added responsibility. Mary and I spoke at some length about our plans for the future; we really wanted to live in Lancashire, which was where we both came from. London was just a huge, strange city to us and Mary was not at ease with the area, which was hardly surprising, considering her experiences to date. But for now, we agreed that the best thing to do was save some money and, in time, apply to transfer north to another prison. We were quietly getting on with our slow but positive plan, when life dealt me yet another losing hand.

It was a Saturday afternoon and, having completed my over-time shift at The Scrubs, I had walked home, changed into casual clothes and taken Mary's dog, Snowy, out for a walk. We had done the usual hundred trees, each getting a proper sniffing from Snowy, when I walked back home with her onto the stairway leading to our apartment. As I looked up, I could see sprawled across the stairs, the same three thugs who had attempted to assault me in The Askew Arms a few months before.

My heart sank; what on earth did these idiots want? I could not for a moment believe they could be so stupid; it had only been weeks since the trial at the Crown Court over their last attack on me and I had been exonerated. There was, in my mind, absolutely no point in me trying to speak to them. So I let the dog go; she legged it for home and I then jumped over the first large lout, hopped to one side, dodging a kick aimed at me, and ran up the stairs, reaching the landing which led to the apartment. However, I had not been quite fast enough and, just as I was heading down the landing, I was pulled back by the young man I knew as LB, the son of the PO, who had hold of my shirt collar.

Snowy the dog was barking like hell and I saw Mary appear in the doorway, holding our baby. I was now struggling with the large lout who had grabbed hold of my head with one arm and was thumping me in the body with his other fist. It took me at least two seconds to force myself free from his grip, but he came at me again, this time throwing a punch aimed at my face; it missed by a millimetre. In that instant, as he lost balance, I spun him round and propelled him head-first into the wall. Stunned, he staggered for a second, then gripping him by his right arm, I locked that securely up his back. He was screaming loudly now as the pain kicked in, but I had no intention of allowing this oversized thug any chance of harming me. With his head under my left arm, I again introduced him with considerable force to the brickwork and heard a satisfyingly solid connection, immediately followed by a really penetrating scream; something was obviously hurting this wannabe bully boy.

The door of our next-door neighbour's apartment suddenly opened and she came running out.

'Call the police,' I said. 'This thug has just assaulted me.'

By this time, LB was slightly subdued but still attempting to break free of my grip, so I applied just a little more pressure to his arm and recognised the groaning as a sign that he knew surrender was now ultimately inevitable.

'Let him go, you bastard!' my next-door neighbour yelled at me. I could hardly believe this. 'Get off him,' she shouted and made a move, as if to physically intervene.

This truly astonished me; here I was, defending myself from an attack by a large lout on my doorstep and the next-door neighbour was about to assist him. Holding the now quiescent LB with his right arm up his back, I used my left hand to point directly at my misguided neighbour and advised the stupid bitch to piss off back inside her hut. It seemed quite a reasonable response at the time.

Poor Mary had been standing in the corridor, watching this horrible incident, and was now beside me, as I maintained my grip on LB. In her arms was our baby, Dulcie Jane. I was concerned; this was a dangerous situation, as the neighbour was still standing in her doorway, appearing quite threatening. I am not sure what Mary said to her but, whatever it was, it worked, as she swiftly retreated, slamming the door shut. Mary then went past me downstairs to a friendly neighbour's home, to telephone the police.

I decided that enough was quite enough and allowed this would-be assailant loose. He was, as far as I could see, shaken but not too badly stirred, I could have damaged him but that would have only made matters worse. I just wanted to be left alone, as did my wife. Pointing to the stairs, I told him to get out and stay out of this building and my life.

Back in our apartment, Mary made me a cup of tea and suggested I calm down. I was really angry at this latest attempt to intimidate and assault me.

'What the hell do they want?' I asked Mary that rhetorical question and then answered it. 'They must want my blood.'

That, though, was not correct, as I was about to discover. When Mary had asked our friendly neighbour downstairs to use her telephone to call the police, she had explained about the woman in the apartment next door and how she had shouted abuse at me. The neighbour had told Mary why the woman was likely taking the side of my assailant. It appeared that her husband had been posted to another Home Office establishment on the other side of London and she was living in that apartment on her own. Over the past six months or so, the young men that had been hanging round the prison quarters causing a nuisance and were regularly seen going in to her flat. The answer as to what this gang of yobbos wanted was not revenge; they wanted access to this middle-aged woman. They had, according to our neighbour, been enjoying her sexual services.

A police officer eventually arrived at our door, some fifteen minutes or so after Mary had called them. I invited the officer in and briefly explained what had happened, gave him some account of the history and asked what the police intended to do. He did say that he would be visiting LB at his home, using the address I had supplied. This was now, in my opinion, becoming a potentially dangerous situation and I told the police officer that, in no uncertain terms. The problem was, as I saw it, that these yahoos had no intention of allowing myself, my wife Mary, and other residents of the complex to live their lives in peace.

After he had gone, Mary told me she wanted us to move away from this place, as it was not safe. Of course, she was right, but what were the options, I wondered. There had to be a way out so I decided that, in the light of this latest assault upon my person, I would submit in writing a request to The Home Office to be relocated to another prison, away from HMP Wormwood Scrubs. To me, it felt like running from a fight I had not started, but having seen how distressed my wife Mary had become, I knew something had to be done.

At The Scrubs on Monday morning at 9am, I knocked on the door of the Number One Chief Officer and was called in. The CO1 read my application for a transfer, which detailed the latest incident, named the culprits responsible and their parents, who were all serving senior staff at The Scrubs. I could hear a sharp intake of breath, then he gave me his best steely-eyed stare.

'You live in prison quarters, don't you, Mr Sutton?' He spoke those words with slow deliberation. I confirmed that, yes, indeed I did.

'Well, if I were you, I'd keep my mouth shut,' he snarled.

This insult to the security of my family from the head of the discipline staff was, for me, one step too far. I had remained as calm, cool and collected as I possibly could under the circumstances, but this enraged me.

'You should be ashamed of yourself,' I said, 'threatening my family, disgraceful.'

I reached across his desk, picked up my written request for a transfer and walked out of the office, straight up the stairs to see The Governor.

My duties continued on C Wing; I was mainly employed patrolling the landings, supervising the serving of meals, general mundane tasks that ensure the day-to-day continuation of service as normal. It was a midweek morning, just before 7am, and I was standing with the other landing officers, waiting for the order to unlock, when I heard a bell ring and a loud banging on a cell door immediately behind me. Then, from within this cell, I heard the most horrific screaming.

It took me just a few seconds to get the door open; when I switched the light on and saw what stood there screaming, a sense of nausea swept through me. Staggering around in the middle of the cell was an elderly thin naked man, smeared from head to foot in blood and gore. It was dribbling down his face in thick dark clots and running across his abdomen in rivulets of crimson red.

'He slit his wrists, Guv!' the inmate shouted, indicating the seemingly lifeless body that lay motionless on the top bunk.

The prisoner had slashed both wrists and remained in his bed, directly above the other occupant of the cell. The blood had pumped out of his body, saturating the mattress and seeping through onto the sleeping prisoner below. I looked and saw that, as the blood had drained through the covers, it had formed long semi-congealed strands; they had trickled slowly all over this man. Someone had sent for the duty Hospital Officer and I did what I could to prevent any further loss of blood, by pressing towels onto the ragged gaping wounds of this inanimate body.

All the time, the screaming continued, as the gore-spattered inmate yelled and cried in terror. The floor was slippery with blood and my hands were covered in it. A few minutes later, the hospital staff arrived and I assisted them in lifting the body down onto a stretcher. Amazingly, the Hospital Officer told me that, in his opinion, the prisoner would survive; he had lost a lot of blood but he was still alive, only just, but he was. I watched as they carried him out, then turning to the naked now silent blood-drenched inmate, I tried to assure him that he was going to be OK.

His bald head was still smeared with dark half-congealed gory crimson clots and he appeared a dreadful sight, but one has to look on the bright side. With a gentle smile, I assured him that, from this day onwards, he was to be officially known as The

Screaming Skull. The landing staff stood laughing loudly at this joke, when The Screaming Skull himself joined in.

'I be OK, Guv,' he said in a cheery cockney accent. 'I robbed all his baccy before I rang me bell.'

That night, when I arrived home from my shift at The Scrubs, Mary said the police had been round to see me and told her they were considering charging my assailant, LB. I had to go and see a certain Sergeant at Ealing Police Station, at my earliest opportunity. I had a quick cup of tea and a cheese sandwich, kissed our baby, Dulcie, and was on my way. It was about time something was done to stop that team of thugs from terrorising the housing complex and assaulting me.

Inside the Police Station, I was taken to an interview room, where an officer took a formal statement from me, which I duly signed. The Sergeant then came in, read what I had written and advised me that the matter was with the duty Police Inspector, who was considering charging LB with assaulting me and/or breach of the peace. They had, he said, already interviewed LB under caution and he was awaiting the decision of the police on action to be taken. This matter was now being dealt with and I would be formally advised, in due course.

The next morning, I was patrolling C Wing, when I heard my name being called over the Tannoy system: 'Mr Sutton, report to the central control unit.' The duty Senior Officer on the desk told me I was wanted by the Number One Chief Officer.

'Who've you hospitalised now?' he jokingly asked, wearing a wry smile.

The too-familiar gruff voice bade me enter, as I knocked on the CO1's office door. For a moment, he just glared at me. 'Go home immediately,' he growled through gritted teeth. 'Get into civilian clothing and report to the Regional Director at the Home Office. Your appointment is at 1:30pm.'

Across his desk, he shoved a large manila envelope with my name on the front. I picked this up and escaped before he could eat me for breakfast.

Mary was surprised to see me returning home so soon and was most intrigued by my summons to see The Regional Director. It was quite unusual for a junior officer to be seen in person by the most senior Home Office official in the South East Prison Service. We both agreed that something serious was about to happen and, as I read the written instructions out loud to her, something flashed before my eyes. For a split second, I had a psychic vision of Strangeways Jail in Manchester.

'Mary, we are going home.'

She looked at me as only someone who has experienced bitter disappointment can. 'John, not with your luck,' she said, giving me an old-fashioned stare.

The Home Office Regional Headquarters for the Prison Service were located in central London, on Queen Anne's Gate close to St. James' Park. I arrived via the Underground railway. Inside the building, I presented my documentation to the security staff and was taken to a waiting room on the sixth floor. I had been there no more than a minute, when a man wearing what looked like an M&S pin-striped suit, walked in.

'Mr Sutton?' I confirmed that I was indeed that man. 'Come with me.'

Inside a rather cluttered office, I stood waiting to discover why I had been summoned by such an august personage as The Regional Director; it didn't take long.

'See that map on the wall?' he said, pointing at a large-scale map of the UK, sporting many small flags. I advised, yes, I could see this. 'Those flags represent Home Office Prison Establishments, prisons. Now go and select one because, on Monday, you are out of HMP Wormwood Scrubs.'

It took me around half a second to reply, 'Strangeways'.

The Regional Director said not another word; he just turned, opened the door and pointed the way out. Something told me that this man had, for whatever reason, taken a disliking to me. It mattered not; I was leaving The Scrubs and would soon be returning home to Lancashire, where Mary and I wanted to be.

All the way back to our apartment I was singing a song to myself: 'I'm Going Home, I've Done My Time…Tie A Yellow Ribbon Round The Old Oak Tree,' etc. I could hardly wait to tell my wife.

CHAPTER 21

STRANGEWAYS JAIL

The news that we were to exit London was welcomed by Mary with great delight. It was 4pm on Thursday; the Regional Director had advised me to be out of The Scrubs by Monday, so I knew I had better get into the jail and sort out the transfer. After a quick cup of tea, I changed into my Prison Officer's uniform and hurried back to The Scrubs. When I walked into the main office, the CO1 was waiting for me.

'My office,' he grunted. I followed him in, closing the door behind me and giving him an understanding little smile. 'You are no longer one of my officers; you are officially transferred to HMP Strangeways, with immediate effect. You are to report there on Monday morning at 09:00 hrs, ready for duty. Now, get out and do not let me see you in this establishment again.'

He handed me another manila envelope, no doubt containing my official notice of transfer. For a brief moment, I looked at the CO1; he was a big old flea-bitten ugly bastard but, right then, I could have kissed him.

'It has been a pleasure to make your acquaintance, Sir,' I said and made a hasty exit.

When I arrived back at Bromyard Avenue and showed Mary my official notification of transfer, she started laughing.

'They obviously want shut of you, John.'

I was glad they did, as where we were right now was unsafe and no one, other than me, had dared to confront the problem. Together, Mary and I took little Dulcie Jane in her pram and walked to the nearest public telephone box, where we called home to The Avenue, Leigh. When we told Mary's mum, Alice, that we were going to be arriving the next day, she was so pleased. Of course we could stay at the house; she would get the room ready at once and everything would be fine.

Mary and I spent that evening packing our belongings into the tea-chests we had stored in the basement unit, from when we had arrived. Less than twelve months we had spent in that apartment, but we had experienced a great deal of anguish during that relatively short time. As we sorted out the suitcases, ready for our escape the next day, I recall wondering what would have happened if I had kept completely away from any kind of confrontation with the louts. It seemed to me that, had no one intervened, they would most certainly have continued to abuse the female occupants of the housing complex. With my wife Mary and new baby, Dulcie Jane, under threat from these yobbos, there seemed no other reasonable course of action.

It wasn't as if I had set out looking for trouble; I had attempted to get the parent of the leading lout to intervene and put a stop to the nonsense. What more could I have done, other than what I was doing now, making an exit? In a way, I was disappointed because, by leaving as we were doing, it was a clear sign to these young thugs that they really could get away with anything. I expressed these thoughts to my wife and she agreed in a way, but wondered why it had to be me. Now, I did not have the answer to that but I knew those louts had not finished with the occupants of this housing complex.

'God help the poor bastards now,' I said to Mary, as we closed the last suitcase and stood it in the hallway, ready for the morning.

I was loading the beat-up old Hillman Imp with our cases, when I saw the postman pass me on the stairs. A thought came into my mind that there was bad news coming. It was as if around that postman there was a darkness that was intended for me. Back in the apartment, I found out that my psychic intuition had been right; there was a formal letter addressed to me, from the local Magistrates Court. My heart sank as soon as I touched that envelope; inside there was a Court Summons. I was to be prosecuted, the summons said, under the Offences Against The Person Act 1861, charged with Common Assault.

I couldn't understand this, how had it happened? The police had assured me they were considering charges against my assailant, LB, and had interviewed him under caution. I had myself been interviewed and given a statement to the police, but not under caution. I showed Mary the court summons and she shook her head.

'I knew it was going too smoothly,' she said and put the kettle on.

Over a cup of hot tea, we both agreed that the only thing we could now do was to again approach the solicitors, Victor Mishcon & Co, seeking their advice.

'When will it all end, John?' Mary asked, holding my hand.

'When the last man is left standing,' I replied and set off to make an appointment to see my lawyer.

At 2pm on that Friday afternoon, I was back in the centre of London, at Victor Mishcon and Co. My solicitor there had agreed to see me as a matter of urgency, to give me advice about the Magistrate's Court summons I had received that morning. This was, he said, a private prosecution, instituted by lawyers acting on behalf of my assailant, LB. The charge against me was one of 'Common Assault' and, if convicted, I could face a term of imprisonment up to six months.

I explained to the solicitor exactly what had happened, told him about the statement I had given to the police and how they had assured me they would be considering prosecuting LB. The facts were, he said, that as a summons had been issued against me by the alleged assailant, it was now up to me to cross-summons him. At first, I couldn't quite understand this; I had thought the police were acting and they would prosecute the thug who had attacked me. It appeared, however, that the lawyers advising him had decided that the best form of defence was attack and they had pre-emptively issued proceedings. This tactic was to force me into a position where I would be facing a trial, no matter what the police did, and from what my solicitor said, he had no faith that they would do anything. The advice he gave me was to instruct Victor Mishcon and Co to issue a counter-summons against the alleged assailant, LB, and get the hearing set down at the Magistrates Court.

This was again going to be at my expense, as there could be no legal aid to support a private action. I had no choice but to agree and signed a letter of instruction, agreeing to pay the costs. I had my cheque book with me and issued them payment on account of £250; this virtually emptied my bank account. This was now way beyond a joke; the invoice for my defence at Knightsbridge Crown Court had not yet arrived and here I was, committing myself to another load of legal costs.

If my wife, Mary, knew how much this bunch of nonsense was costing, she would have had a duck fit. I spent the next hour with a solicitor's clerk, making a full and comprehensive statement. As I recounted what had happened, it struck me that this was all a deliberate ploy to price me out of the proceedings. By the time I finished giving my statement, it was 4pm and I had to get back across London in the rush hour to Mary, who was waiting for me with Dulcie, to start our escape from the Big Smoke.

After hours of bumper-to bumper-traffic on the way to the M1 motorway and two hundred miles of hard road, we finally arrived at The Avenue, Leigh, just before midnight. Mary's mum and dad were waiting up for us and Dulcie Jane was soon being cuddled and kissed by her nan. Thankfully, the bedroom was ready, with a hot water bottle in the bed to make it nice and warm. Within seconds of my head hitting the pillow, I was asleep.

I did not awaken till gone 9am, by which time, Mary and Dulcie were up, dressed and ready to go shopping. We were home in Lancashire, but I still had unfinished business in London. The solicitor had assured me they would be proceeding with the issuing of a counter-summons and have the case set down for hearing early in the new year, something to look forward to.

Sunday morning, we decided to visit my grandparents at Foulridge near Colne, on the Lancashire and Yorkshire border. It was a cold early December day, heavy grey skies with the threat of snow in the air. I took my time driving there along familiar roads, through the old industrial towns of Bolton, Burnley and Nelson. As we passed row after row of dark brick terraced houses and many closed and decrepit cotton mills, I thought back to my days as a weaver, when I was just sixteen years of age. The noise in those old weaving sheds was intense, the atmosphere damp and thick with cotton dust. Long shifts working at the Lancashire and Northrop looms, 6am to 2pm or 2pm to 10pm, it was hard labour but the people there loved their work and were proud of the cloth they wove.

Mill after mill we drove past; they were empty and still. This was all that remained of the Lancashire cotton trade. Big brick-built mills, fast fading monuments with their towering soot-stained chimneys and forever silent sheds. Down the many cobbled side streets, where once the clog-wearing weavers had clattered along on their way to work; they were only memories now. I and my grandparents before me, my mother too, were a part of those memories, when Lancashire mills had woven the cloth that clothed the world.

Cromwell Street in Foulridge consists of a long row of late 17th century stone cottages. My grandparents, Billy and Eva Walsh, lived in number four. There were ancient exposed oak beams, two-foot-thick solid stone walls, an open fire, stone steps leading down to a dark cellar and my beloved Grandma and Granddad. They were really pleased to see us and Grandma was thrilled to be holding her little princess again. After a nice cup of strong tea and a long talk about what was happening in the village, i.e. not a lot, I decided to spend a few moments visiting the cellar. It had been my favourite place when I was a little boy and, for me, it held a certain magic, as it was there I first encountered what I now knew to be a ghost.

The well-worn stone steps leading down to the cellar of 4

Cromwell Street led me into what had been the coal storage area. From there, I walked through to the main cellar, which looked unchanged, full of cobwebs and dark shadows. I took a few careful steps forward and discovered that the old carved oak stool I used to sit on was still there. It seemed a bit small for me now but I sat down on it and thought back to the time I had been there as a boy. The light filtering in through the murky window at the far end of the cellar did not quite reach where I was now sitting.

This was the haunted corner where, over twenty years before, I had heard the voice of a long-ago man speaking to me. I wondered, was his spirit still around and, for a moment, closed my eyes and allowed my senses to receive whatever was within this ancient cellar. There came an almost silent rustling in the corner directly behind me and I felt a sudden coldness brush against my chest. Opening my eyes, I saw that the long ashen grey cobwebs hanging from the oak beams were shifting slowly, as if blown by a gentle breeze.

'John.' A voice I almost recognised spoke my name, but there was no one there.

I looked more closely into the shadows and saw something shining blue, slightly hidden by a split wooden brush on the cold stone floor. I reached out to see what this was and found it to be a badly bent toy tin train that I seemed to remember having seen before. Examining this, I noticed the little tin train driver had been bent over and, in that second, I recalled a young boy doing this; I was that boy. The tin train; I had not seen it since I was around seven years of age.

'John.' I heard the voice again speaking my name, though it seemed farther away now. 'John, are you asleep?' I looked up to see Mary by my side, with a concerned smile on her face. 'You've been down here almost an hour, are you OK' she asked.

To me, it had seemed only minutes. I told her I was fine and was going to show her my old toy train, but when I looked, it was not to be found. Where it had been, there was only dust and a broken broom.

That Sunday night, in bed at Mary's parent's house, on The Avenue in Leigh, I could not get to sleep. Thoughts of what I had experienced at The Scrubs kept running through my mind and I could not expel them. There was the forthcoming court case to deal with, the problems I was certain to face, paying the solicitors' fees, the fact we were homeless and our beautiful baby girl needed extra special care. I thought back to what Mary had told me just two years before, when she had been to see the psychic medium, Lillian Hill, for a clairvoyant reading. She had predicted I would face a series of terrible struggles and be subjected to attack after attack. So far, Mrs Hill had been right; it had been tough and, if I was climbing a golden ladder, as she said, I was currently standing on the bottom rung.

Poor Mary, asleep by my side; she did not know that I owed legal costs running into the thousands. We were significantly worse off financially than we had been two years before, when I had first applied to join The Prison Service. Tomorrow, I had to start all over again at Strangeways and was certain someone had made a call, marking my card. Or was I becoming paranoid, had I started to imagine problems that did not exist? Across the room, safe within her cot, little Dulcie Jane was in the land of dreams, a wonderful place to be, I thought, turning and restlessly turning, until night slowly became day.

Monday morning was wet and windy, blowing my car about as I drove down the A580, known as The East Lancs Road, into central Manchester. Passing through Irlam of The Heights, I could see the tall dark tower of Strangeways jail, pointing like an accusing finger at the sky. It really was a horrible blot on an already austere industrial landscape. Walking up to the prison, I stopped for a moment to look at the entrance. Two dark red brick towers stood on either side of the huge oak and iron gates, giving it an imposing, almost intimidating presence. On that bleak rain-swept morning, with heavy grey clouds louring in the sky, HMP Strangeways loomed like some mediaeval castle from a gothic horror movie.

I knew the prison officer that opened the gate; it was Joe the ex-coalman and he, of course, remembered me from our time in the training school together. Joe gave me a rather troubled stare and I sensed he had heard something about why I was being transferred from The Scrubs.

'They're expecting you, John,' he said, then in a dark tone, slightly above a whisper, added, 'Whatever you did, it has upset a lot of people.'

As he slammed the gate shut, the dull thudding sound echoed ominously around the grim Victorian gatehouse of Strangeways jail.

THE END

HMP MANCHESTER PRISON OFFICER Part 2 will be available from this publisher in 2023. You can watch John Sutton's YouTube interview on Shaun Attwood's channel by searching for Freemason Prison Officers v Manchester Guard: John Sutton Podcast 337

ABOUT THE AUTHOR

John G Sutton is an internationally published bestselling author, a poet, songwriter and professional psychic consultant. John was, for 27 years, the feature editor of the monthly journal of Spiritualism 'Psychic World', in which he wrote a column. His recent credits include 'Psychic Pets', published by Bloomsbury, 'The Psychic World of Derek Acorah', published by Piatkus, 'Animals Make You Feel Better', published by Element/Penguin. John is the web-master of the highly rated website www.psychicworld.net. John's highly rated YouTube channel 'Tales From The Jails' features John discussing all matters pertaining to prisons.

Born in Lancashire in 1949, John was half-educated in the town of Leigh, where one of his teachers was the Oscar-winning screenwriter, Colin Welland. Following five years' service in HM Forces as an NCO, John joined HM Prison Service in January 1975, at Strangeways Jail in Manchester. This book tells the true story of what happened next.

John G Sutton now lives in his native Lancashire with his wife, Mary, whom he married on his 21st birthday in August 1970. Their only child, Dulcie Jane, lives close by with her husband Robert and their two wonderful children, Aaron and Jasper, who call John 'Grandpa Grumps'.

OTHER BOOKS BY GADFLY PRESS

By William Rodríguez Abadía:
Son of the Cali Cartel: The Narcos Who Wiped Out Pablo Escobar and the Medellín Cartel

By Chet Sandhu:
Self-Made, Dues Paid: An Asian Kid Who Became an International Drug-Smuggling Gangster

By Kaz B:
Confessions of a Dominatrix: My Secret BDSM Life

By Peter McAleese:
Killing Escobar and Soldier Stories

By Joe Egan:
Big Joe Egan: The Toughest White Man on the Planet

By Anthony Valentine:
Britain's No. 1 Art Forger Max Brandrett: The Life of a Cheeky Faker

By Johnnyboy Steele:
Scotland's Johnnyboy: The Bird That Never Flew

By Ian 'Blink' MacDonald:
Scotland's Wildest Bank Robber: Guns, Bombs and Mayhem in Glasgow's Gangland

By Michael Sheridan:
The Murder of Sophie:
How I Hunted and Haunted the West Cork Killer

By Steve Wraith:
The Krays' Final Years: My Time with London's Most Iconic
Gangsters

By Natalie Welsh:
Escape from Venezuela's Deadliest Prison

By Shaun Attwood:
English Shaun Trilogy
Party Time
Hard Time
Prison Time

War on Drugs Series
Pablo Escobar: Beyond Narcos
American Made: Who Killed Barry Seal? Pablo Escobar or George
HW Bush
The Cali Cartel: Beyond Narcos
Clinton Bush and CIA Conspiracies: From the Boys on the Tracks to
Jeffrey Epstein
Who Killed Epstein? Prince Andrew or Bill Clinton

Un-Making a Murderer:
The Framing of Steven Avery and Brendan Dassey
The Mafia Philosopher: Two Tonys
Life Lessons

Pablo Escobar's Story (4-book series)

By Johnnyboy Steele:

Scotland's Johnnyboy: The Bird That Never Flew

"A cross between *Shawshank Redemption* and *Escape from Alcatraz*!" – Shaun Attwood, YouTuber and Author

All his life, 'Johnnyboy' Steele has been running. Firstly, from an abusive father, then from the rigours of an approved school and a young offenders jail, and, finally, from the harshness of adult prison. This book details how the Steele brothers staged the most daring breakout that Glasgow's Barlinnie prison had ever seen and recounts what happened when their younger brother, Joseph, was falsely accused of the greatest mass murder in Scottish legal history.

If Johnnyboy had wings, he would have flown to help his family, but he would have to wait for freedom to use his expertise to publicise young Joe's miscarriage of justice.

This is a compelling, often shocking and uncompromisingly honest account of how the human spirit can survive against almost crushing odds. It is a story of family love, friendship and, ultimately, a desire for justice.

By Ian 'Blink' Macdonald:

Scotland's Wildest Bank Robber: Guns, Bombs and Mayhem in Glasgow's Gangland

As a young man in Glasgow's underworld, Ian 'Blink' MacDonald earned a reputation for fighting and stabbing his enemies. After refusing to work for Arthur "The Godfather" Thompson, he attempted to steal £6 million in a high-risk armed bank robbery. While serving 16 years, Blink met the torture-gang boss Eddie Richardson, the serial killer Archie Hall, notorious lifer Charles Bronson and members of the Krays.

After his release, his drug-fuelled violent lifestyle created conflict with the police and rival gangsters. Rearrested several times, he was the target of a gruesome assassination attempt. During filming for Danny Dyer's Deadliest Men, a bomb was discovered under Blink's car and the terrified camera crew members fled from Scotland.

In *Scotland's Wildest Bank Robber*, Blink provides an eye-opening account of how he survived gangland warfare, prisons, stabbings and bombs.

By Michael Sheridan:

The Murder of Sophie: How I Hunted and Haunted the West Cork Killer

Just before Christmas, 1996, a beautiful French woman – the wife of a movie mogul – was brutally murdered outside of her holiday home in a remote region of West Cork, Ireland. The crime was reported by a local journalist, Ian Bailey, who was at the forefront of the case until he became the prime murder suspect. Arrested twice, he was released without charge.

This was the start of a saga lasting decades with twists and turns and a battle for justice in two countries, which culminated in the 2019 conviction of Bailey – in his absence – by the French Criminal court in Paris. But it was up to the Irish courts to decide whether he would be extradited to serve a 25-year prison sentence.

With the unrivalled co-operation of major investigation sources and the backing of the victim's family, the author unravels the shocking facts of a unique murder case.

By Steve Wraith:

The Krays' Final Years:
My Time with London's Most Iconic Gangsters

Britain's most notorious twins – Ron and Reg Kray – ascended the underworld to become the most feared and legendary gangsters in London. Their escalating mayhem culminated in murder, for which they received life sentences in 1969.

While incarcerated, they received letters from a schoolboy from Tyneside, Steve Wraith, who was mesmerised by their story. Eventually, Steve visited them in prison and a friendship formed. The Twins hired Steve as an unofficial advisor, which brought him into contact with other members of their crime family. At Ron's funeral, Steve was Charlie Kray's right-hand man.

Steve documents Ron's time in Broadmoor – a high-security psychiatric hospital – where he was battling insanity and heavily medicated. Steve details visiting Reg, who served almost 30 years in a variety of prisons, where the gangster was treated with the utmost respect by the staff and the inmates.

By Natalie Welsh:

Escape from Venezuela's Deadliest Prison

After getting arrested at a Venezuelan airport with a suitcase of cocaine, Natalie was clueless about the danger she was facing. Sentenced to 10 years, she arrived at a prison with armed men on the roof, whom she mistakenly believed were the guards, only to find out they were homicidal gang members. Immediately, she was plunged into a world of unimaginable horror and escalating violence, where murder, rape and all-out gang warfare were carried out with the complicity of corrupt guards. Male prisoners often entered the women's housing area, bringing gunfire with them and leaving corpses behind. After 4.5 years, Natalie risked everything to escape and flee through Colombia, with the help of a guard who had fallen deeply in love with her.

By Shaun Attwood:

Pablo Escobar: Beyond Narcos

War on Drugs Series Book 1

The mind-blowing true story of Pablo Escobar and the Medellín Cartel, beyond their portrayal on Netflix.

Colombian drug lord Pablo Escobar was a devoted family man and a psychopathic killer; a terrible enemy, yet a wonderful friend. While donating millions to the poor, he bombed and tortured his enemies – some had their eyeballs removed with hot spoons. Through ruthless cunning and America's insatiable appetite for cocaine, he became a multi-billionaire, who lived in a $100-million house with its own zoo.

Pablo Escobar: Beyond Narcos demolishes the standard good versus evil telling of his story. The authorities were not hunting Pablo down to stop his cocaine business. They were taking it over.

American Made: Who Killed Barry Seal?
Pablo Escobar or George HW Bush

War on Drugs Series Book 2

Set in a world where crime and government coexist, *American Made* is the jaw-dropping true story of CIA pilot Barry Seal that the Hollywood movie starring Tom Cruise is afraid to tell.

Barry Seal flew cocaine and weapons worth billions of dollars into and out of America in the 1980s. After he became a government informant, Pablo Escobar's Medellin Cartel offered a million for him alive and half a million dead. But his real trouble began after he threatened to expose the dirty dealings of George HW Bush.

American Made rips the roof off Bush and Clinton's complicity in cocaine trafficking in Mena, Arkansas.

"A conspiracy of the grandest magnitude." Congressman Bill Alexander on the Mena affair.

The Cali Cartel: Beyond Narcos

War on Drugs Series Book 3

An electrifying account of the Cali Cartel, beyond its portrayal on Netflix.

From the ashes of Pablo Escobar's empire rose an even bigger and more malevolent cartel. A new breed of sophisticated mobsters became the kings of cocaine. Their leader was Gilberto Rodríguez Orejuela – known as the Chess Player, due to his foresight and calculated cunning.

Gilberto and his terrifying brother, Miguel, ran a multi-billion-dollar drug empire like a corporation. They employed a politically astute brand of thuggery and spent $10 million to put a president in power. Although the godfathers from Cali preferred bribery over violence, their many loyal torturers and hitmen were never idle.

Clinton, Bush and CIA Conspiracies: From the Boys on the Tracks to Jeffrey Epstein

War on Drugs Series Book 4

In the 1980s, George HW Bush imported cocaine to finance an illegal war in Nicaragua. Governor Bill Clinton's Arkansas state police provided security for the drug drops. For assisting the CIA, the Clinton Crime Family was awarded the White House. The #clintonbodycount continues to this day, with the deceased including Jeffrey Epstein.

This book features harrowing true stories that reveal the insanity of the drug war. A mother receives the worst news about her son. A journalist gets a tip that endangers his life. An unemployed man becomes California's biggest crack dealer. A DEA agent in Mexico is sacrificed for going after the big players.

The lives of Linda Ives, Gary Webb, Freeway Rick Ross and Kiki Camarena are shattered by brutal experiences. Not all of them will survive.

Pablo Escobar's Story (4-book series)

"Finally, the definitive book about Escobar, original and up-to-date." – UNILAD

"The most comprehensive account ever written." – True Geordie

Pablo Escobar was a mama's boy, who cherished his family and sang in the shower, yet he bombed a passenger plane and formed a death squad that used genital electrocution.

Most Escobar biographies only provide a few pieces of the puzzle, but this action-packed 1000-page book reveals everything about the king of cocaine.

Mostly translated from Spanish, Part 1 contains stories untold in the English-speaking world, including:

The tragic death of his youngest brother, Fernando.

The fate of his pregnant mistress.

The shocking details of his affair with a TV celebrity.

The presidential candidate who encouraged him to eliminate their rivals.

The Mafia Philosopher

"A fast-paced true-crime memoir with all of the action of Goodfellas." – UNILAD

"Sopranos v Sons of Anarchy with an Alaskan-snow backdrop." – True Geordie Podcast

Breaking bones, burying bodies and planting bombs became second nature to Two Tonys, while working for the Bonanno Crime Family, whose exploits inspired The Godfather.

After a dispute with an outlaw motorcycle club, Two Tonys left a trail of corpses from Arizona to Alaska. On the run, he was pursued by bikers and a neo-Nazi gang, blood-thirsty for revenge, while a homicide detective launched a nationwide manhunt.

As the mist from his smoking gun fades, readers are left with an unexpected portrait of a stoic philosopher with a wealth of charm, a glorious turn of phrase and a fanatical devotion to his daughter.

Party Time

An action-packed roller-coaster account of a life spiralling out of control, featuring wild women, gangsters and a mountain of drugs.

Shaun Attwood arrived in Phoenix, Arizona, a penniless business graduate from a small industrial town in England. Within a decade, he became a stock-market millionaire. But he was leading a double life.

After taking his first ecstasy pill at a rave in Manchester as a shy student, Shaun became intoxicated by the party lifestyle that would change his fortune. Years later, in the Arizona desert, he became submerged in a criminal underworld, throwing parties for thousands of ravers and running an ecstasy ring in competition with the Mafia mass murderer, Sammy 'The Bull' Gravano.

As greed and excess tore through his life, Shaun had

eye-watering encounters with Mafia hitmen and crystal-meth addicts, enjoyed extravagant debauchery with superstar DJs and glitter girls, and ingested enough drugs to kill a herd of elephants. This is his story.

Hard Time

"Makes the Shawshank Redemption look like a holiday camp." – NOTW

After a SWAT team smashed down stock-market millionaire Shaun Attwood's door, he found himself inside Arizona's deadliest jail and locked into a brutal struggle for survival.

Shaun's hope of living the American Dream turned into a nightmare of violence and chaos, when he had a run-in with Sammy "the Bull" Gravano, an Italian Mafia mass murderer.

In jail, Shaun was forced to endure cockroaches crawling in his ears at night, dead rats in the food and the sound of skulls getting cracked against toilets. He meticulously documented the conditions and smuggled out his message.

Join Shaun on a harrowing voyage into the darkest recesses of human existence.

Hard Time provides a revealing glimpse into the tragedy, brutality, dark comedy and eccentricity of prison life.

Featured worldwide on Nat Geo Channel's Locked-Up/Banged-Up Abroad Raving Arizona.

Prison Time

Sentenced to 9½ years in Arizona's state prison for distributing ecstasy, Shaun finds himself living among gang members, sexual predators and drug-crazed psychopaths. After being attacked by a Californian biker, in for stabbing a girlfriend, Shaun writes about the prisoners who befriend, protect and inspire him. They include T-Bone, a massive African American ex-Marine, who risks his life saving vulnerable inmates from rape, and Two Tonys, an old-school Mafia murderer, who left the corpses of his rivals from Arizona to Alaska. They teach Shaun how to turn incarceration to his advantage, and to learn from his mistakes.

Shaun is no stranger to love and lust in the heterosexual world, but the tables are turned on him inside. Sexual advances come at him from all directions, some cleverly disguised, others more sinister – making Shaun question his sexual identity.

Resigned to living alongside violent, mentally ill and drug-addicted inmates, Shaun immerses himself in psychology and philosophy, to try to make sense of his past behaviour, and begins applying what he learns, as he adapts to prison life. Encouraged by Two Tonys to explore fiction as well, Shaun reads over 1000 books which, with support from a brilliant psychotherapist, Dr Owen, speed along his personal development. As his ability to deflect daily threats improves, Shaun begins to look forward to his release with optimism and a new love waiting for him. Yet the words of Aristotle from one of Shaun's books will prove prophetic: "We cannot learn without pain."

Un-Making a Murderer: The Framing of Steven Avery and Brendan Dassey

Innocent people do go to jail. Sometimes mistakes are made. But even more terrifying is when the authorities conspire to frame them. That's what happened to Steven Avery and Brendan Dassey, who were convicted of murder and are serving life sentences.

Un-Making a Murderer is an explosive book, which uncovers the illegal, devious and covert tactics used by Wisconsin officials, including:

– Concealing Other Suspects

– Paying Expert Witnesses to Lie

– Planting Evidence

– Jury Tampering

The art of framing innocent people has been in practice for centuries and will continue until the perpetrators are held accountable. Turning conventional assumptions and beliefs in the justice system upside down, *Un-Making a Murderer* takes you on that journey.

HARD TIME BY SHAUN ATTWOOD

CHAPTER 1

Sleep deprived and scanning for danger, I enter a dark cell on the second floor of the maximum-security Madison Street jail in Phoenix, Arizona, where guards and gang members are murdering prisoners. Behind me, the metal door slams heavily. Light slants into the cell through oblong gaps in the door, illuminating a prisoner cocooned in a white sheet, snoring lightly on the top bunk about two thirds of the way up the back wall. Relieved there is no immediate threat, I place my mattress on the grimy floor. Desperate to rest, I notice movement on the cement-block walls. *Am I hallucinating?* I blink several times. The walls appear to ripple. Stepping closer, I see the walls are alive with insects. I flinch. So many are swarming, I wonder if they're a colony of ants on the move. To get a better look, I put my eyes right up to them. They are mostly the size of almonds and have antennae. American cockroaches. I've seen them in the holding cells downstairs in smaller numbers, but nothing like this. A chill spread over my body. I back away.

Something alive falls from the ceiling and bounces off the base of my neck. I jump. With my night vision improving, I spot cockroaches weaving in and out of the base of the fluorescent strip light. Every so often one drops onto the concrete and resumes crawling. Examining the bottom bunk, I realise why my cellmate is sleeping at a higher elevation: cockroaches are pouring from gaps in the decrepit wall at the level of my bunk. The area is thick with them. Placing my mattress on the bottom bunk scatters them. I walk towards the toilet, crunching a few under my shower sandals. I urinate and grab the toilet roll. A cockroach darts from the centre of the roll onto my hand, tickling my fingers. My arm jerks as if it has a mind of its own, losing the cockroach and the toilet roll. Using a towel, I wipe the bulk of them off the bottom bunk, stopping only to shake the odd one off my hand. I unroll my mattress. They begin to regroup and inhabit my mattress. My adrenaline is pumping so much, I lose my fatigue.

Nauseated, I sit on a tiny metal stool bolted to the wall. *How will I sleep? How's my cellmate sleeping through the infestation and my arrival?* Copying his technique, I cocoon myself in a sheet and lie down, crushing more cockroaches. The only way they can access me now is through the breathing hole I've left in the sheet by the lower half of my face. Inhaling their strange musty odour, I close my eyes. I can't sleep. I feel them crawling on the sheet around my feet. *Am I imagining things?* Frightened of them infiltrating my breathing hole, I keep opening my eyes. Cramps cause me to rotate onto my other side. Facing the wall, I'm repulsed by so many of them just inches away. I return to my original side.

The sheet traps the heat of the Sonoran Desert to my body, soaking me in sweat. Sweat tickles my body, tricking my mind into thinking the cockroaches are infiltrating and crawling on me. The trapped heat aggravates my bleeding skin infections and bedsores. I want to scratch myself, but I know better. The outer layers of my skin have turned soggy from sweating constantly in this concrete oven. Squirming on the bunk fails to stop the relentless itchiness of my skin. Eventually, I scratch myself. Clumps of moist skin detach under my nails. Every now and then I become so uncomfortable, I must open my cocoon to waft the heat out, which allows the cockroaches in. It takes hours to drift to sleep. I only manage a few hours. I awake stuck to the soaked sheet, disgusted by the cockroach carcasses compressed against the mattress.

The cockroaches plague my new home until dawn appears at the dots in the metal grid over a begrimed strip of four-inch-thick bullet-proof glass at the top of the back wall – the cell's only source of outdoor light. They disappear into the cracks in the walls, like vampire mist retreating from sunlight. But not all of them. There were so many on the night shift that even their vastly reduced number is too many to dispose of. And they act like they know it. They roam around my feet with attitude, as if to make it clear that I'm trespassing on their turf.

My next set of challenges will arise not from the insect world, but from my neighbours. I'm the new arrival, subject to scrutiny about my charges just like when I'd run into the Aryan Brotherhood prison gang on my first day at the medium-security Towers jail a year ago. I wish my cellmate would wake up, brief me on the mood of the locals and introduce me to the head of the white gang. No such luck. Chow is announced over a speaker system in a crackly robotic voice, but he doesn't stir.

I emerge into the day room for breakfast. Prisoners in black-and-white bee-striped uniforms gather under the metal-grid stairs and tip dead cockroaches into a trash bin from plastic peanut-butter containers they'd set as traps during the night. All eyes are on me in the chow line. Watching who sits where, I hold my head up, put on a solid stare and pretend to be as at home in this environment as the cockroaches. It's all an act. I'm lonely and afraid. I loathe having to explain myself to the head of the white race, who I assume is the toughest murderer. I've been in jail long enough to know that taking my breakfast to my cell will imply that I have something to hide.

The gang punishes criminals with certain charges. The most serious are sex offenders, who are KOS: Kill On Sight. Other charges are punishable by SOS – Smash On Sight – such as drive-by shootings because women and kids sometimes get killed. It's called convict justice. Gang members are constantly looking for people to beat up because that's how they earn their reputations and tattoos. The most serious acts of violence earn the highest-ranking tattoos. To be a full gang member requires murder. I've observed the body language and techniques inmates trying to integrate employ. An inmate with a spring in his step and an air of confidence is likely to be accepted. A person who avoids eye contact and fails to introduce himself to the gang is likely to be preyed on. Some of the failed attempts I saw ended up with heads getting cracked against toilets, a sound I've grown familiar with. I've seen prisoners being extracted on stretchers who looked dead – one had yellow fluid leaking from his head. The constant violence gives me nightmares, but the reality is that I put myself in here, so I force myself to accept it as a part of my punishment.

It's time to apply my knowledge. With a self-assured stride, I take my breakfast bag to the table of white inmates covered in neo-Nazi tattoos, allowing them to question me.

"Mind if I sit with you guys?" I ask, glad exhaustion has deepened my voice.

"These seats are taken. But you can stand at the corner of the table."

The man who answered is probably the head of the gang. I size him up. Cropped brown hair. A dangerous glint in Nordic-blue eyes. Tiny pupils that suggest he's on heroin. Weightlifter-type veins bulging from a sturdy neck. Political ink on arms crisscrossed with scars. About the same age as me, thirty-three.

"Thanks. I'm Shaun from England." I volunteer my origin to show I'm different from them but not in a way that might get me smashed.

"I'm Bullet, the head of the whites." He offers me his fist to bump. "Where you roll in from, wood?"

Addressing me as wood is a good sign. It's what white gang members on a friendly basis call each other.

"Towers jail. They increased my bond and re-classified me to maximum security."

"What's your bond at?"

"I've got two $750,000 bonds," I say in a monotone. This is no place to brag about bonds.

"How many people you kill, brother?" His eyes drill into mine, checking whether my body language supports my story. My body language so far is spot on.

"None. I threw rave parties. They got us talking about drugs on wiretaps." Discussing drugs on the phone does not warrant a $1.5 million bond. I know and beat him to his next question. "Here's my charges." I show him my charge sheet, which includes conspiracy and leading a crime syndicate – both from running an Ecstasy ring.

Bullet snatches the paper and scrutinises it. Attempting to pre-empt his verdict, the other whites study his face. On edge, I wait for him to respond. Whatever he says next will determine whether I'll be accepted or victimised.

"Are you some kind of jailhouse attorney?" Bullet asks. "I want someone to read through my case paperwork." During our few minutes of conversation, Bullet has seen through my act and concluded that I'm educated – a possible resource to him.

I appreciate that he'll accept me if I take the time to read his case. "I'm no jailhouse attorney, but I'll look through it and help you however I can."

"Good. I'll stop by your cell later on, wood."

After breakfast, I seal as many of the cracks in the walls as I can with toothpaste. The cell smells minty, but the cockroaches still find their way in. Their day shift appears to be collecting information on the brown paper bags under my bunk, containing a few items of food that I purchased from the commissary; bags that I tied off with rubber bands in the hope of keeping the cockroaches out. Relentlessly, the cockroaches explore the bags for entry points, pausing over and probing the most worn and vulnerable regions. *Will the nightly swarm eat right through the paper?* I read all morning, wondering whether my cellmate has died in his cocoon, his occasional breathing sounds reassuring me.

Bullet stops by late afternoon and drops his case paperwork off. He's been charged with Class 3 felonies and less, not serious crimes, but is facing a double-digit sentence because of his prior convictions and Security Threat Group status in the prison system. The proposed sentencing range seems disproportionate. I'll advise him to reject the plea bargain – on the assumption he already knows to do so, but is just seeking the comfort of a second opinion, like many un-sentenced inmates. When he returns for his paperwork, our conversation disturbs my cellmate – the cocoon shuffles – so we go upstairs to his cell. I tell Bullet what I think. He is excitable, a different man from earlier, his pupils almost non-existent.

"This case ain't shit. But my prosecutor knows I done other shit, all kinds of heavy shit, but can't prove it. I'd do anything to get that sorry bitch off my fucking ass. She's asking for something bad to happen to her. Man, if I ever get bonded out, I'm gonna chop that bitch into pieces. Kill her slowly though. Like to work her over with a blowtorch."

Such talk can get us both charged with conspiring to murder a prosecutor, so I try to steer him elsewhere. "It's crazy how they can catch you doing one thing, yet try to sentence you for all of the things they think you've ever done."

"Done plenty. Shot some dude in the stomach once. Rolled him up in a blanket and threw him in a dumpster."

Discussing past murders is as unsettling as future ones. "So, what's all your tattoos mean, Bullet? Like that eagle on your chest?"

"Why you wanna know?" Bullet's eyes probe mine.

My eyes hold their ground. "Just curious."

"It's a war bird. The AB patch."

"AB patch?"

"What the Aryan Brotherhood gives you when you've put enough work in."

"How long does it take to earn a patch?"

"Depends how quickly you put your work in. You have to earn your lightning bolts first."

"Why you got red and black lightning bolts?"

"You get SS bolts for beating someone down or for being an enforcer for the family. Red lightning bolts for killing someone. I was sent down as a youngster. They gave me steel and told me who to handle and I handled it. You don't ask questions. You just get blood on your steel. Dudes who get these tats without putting work in are told to cover them up or leave the yard."

"What if they refuse?"

"They're held down and we carve the ink off them."

Imagining them carving a chunk of flesh to remove a tattoo, I cringe. He's really enjoying telling me this now. His volatile nature is clear and frightening. *He's accepted me too much. He's trying to impress me before making demands.*

At night, I'm unable to sleep. Cocooned in heat, surrounded by cockroaches, I hear the swamp-cooler vent – a metal grid at the top of a wall – hissing out tepid air. Giving up on sleep, I put my earphones on and tune into National Public Radio. Listening to a Vivaldi violin concerto, I close my eyes and press my tailbone down to straighten my back as if I'm doing a yogic relaxation. The playful allegro thrills me, lifting my spirits, but the wistful adagio provokes sad emotions and tears. I open my eyes and gaze into the gloom. Due to lack of sleep, I start hallucinating and hearing voices over the music whispering threats. I'm at breaking point. Although I have accepted that I committed crimes and deserve to be punished, no one should have to live like this. I'm furious at myself for making the series of reckless decisions that put me in here and for losing absolutely everything. As violins crescendo in my ears, I remember what my life used to be like.

PRISON TIME BY SHAUN ATTWOOD

CHAPTER 1

"I've got a padlock in a sock. I can smash your brains in while you're asleep. I can kill you whenever I want." My new cellmate sizes me up with no trace of human feeling in his eyes. Muscular and pot-bellied, he's caked in prison ink, including six snakes on his skull, slithering side by side. The top of his right ear is missing in a semi-circle.

The waves of fear are overwhelming. After being in transportation all day, I can feel my bladder hurting. "I'm not looking to cause any trouble. I'm the quietest cellmate you'll ever have. All I do is read and write."

Scowling, he shakes his head. "Why've they put a fish in with me?" He swaggers close enough for me to smell his cigarette breath. "Us convicts don't get along with fresh fish."

"Should I ask to move then?" I say, hoping he'll agree if he hates new prisoners so much.

"No! They'll think I threatened you!"

In the eight by twelve feet slab of space, I swerve around him and place my property box on the top bunk.

He pushes me aside and grabs the box. "You just put that on my artwork! I ought to fucking smash you, fish!"

"Sorry, I didn't see it."

"You need to be more aware of your fucking surroundings! What you in for anyway, fish?"

I explain my charges, Ecstasy dealing and how I spent twenty-six months fighting my case.

"How come the cops were so hard-core after you?" he asks, squinting.

"It was a big case, a multi-million-dollar investigation. They raided over a hundred people and didn't find any drugs. They were pretty pissed off. I'd stopped dealing by the time they caught up with me, but I'd done plenty over the years, so I accept my punishment."

"Throwing raves," he says, staring at the ceiling as if remembering something. "Were you partying with underage girls?" he asks, his voice slow, coaxing.

Being called a sex offender is the worst insult in prison. Into my third year of incarceration, I'm conditioned to react. "What you trying to say?" I yell angrily, brow clenched.

"Were you fucking underage girls?" Flexing his body, he shakes both fists as if about to punch me.

"Hey, I'm no child molester, and I'd prefer you didn't say shit like that!"

"My buddy next door is doing twenty-five to life for murdering a child molester. How do I know Ecstasy dealing ain't your cover story?" He inhales loudly, nostrils flaring.

"You want to see my fucking paperwork?"

A stocky prisoner walks in. Short hair. Dark eyes. Powerful neck. On one arm: a tattoo of a man in handcuffs above the word OMERTA – the Mafia code of silence towards law enforcement. "What the fuck's going on in here, Bud?" asks Junior Bull – the son of "Sammy the Bull" Gravano, the Mafia mass murderer who was my biggest competitor in the Ecstasy market.

Relieved to see a familiar face, I say, "How're you doing?"

Shaking my hand, he says in a New York Italian accent, "I'm doing alright. I read that shit in the newspaper about you starting a blog in Sheriff Joe Arpaio's jail."

"The blog's been bringing media heat on the conditions."

"You know him?" Bud asks.

"Yeah, from Towers jail. He's a good dude. He's in for dealing Ecstasy like me."

"It's a good job you said that 'cause I was about to smash his ass," Bud says.

"It's a good job Wild Man ain't here 'cause you'd a got your ass thrown off the balcony," Junior Bull says.

I laugh. The presence of my best friend, Wild Man, was partly the reason I never took a beating at the county jail, but with Wild Man in a different prison, I feel vulnerable. When Bud casts a death stare on me, my smile fades.

"What the fuck you guys on about?" Bud asks.

"Let's go talk downstairs." Junior Bull leads Bud out.

I rush to a stainless-steel sink/toilet bolted to a cement-block wall by the front of the cell, unbutton my orange jumpsuit and crane my neck to watch the upper-tier walkway in case Bud returns. I bask in relief as my bladder deflates. After flushing, I take stock of my new home, grateful for the slight improvement in the conditions versus what I'd grown accustomed to in Sheriff Joe Arpaio's jail. No cockroaches. No blood stains. A working swamp cooler. Something I've never seen in a cell before: shelves. The steel table bolted to the wall is slightly larger, too. *But how will I concentrate on writing with Bud around?* There's a mixture of smells in the room. Cleaning chemicals. Aftershave. Tobacco. A vinegar-like odour. The slit of a window at the back overlooks gravel in a no-man's-land before the next building with gleaming curls of razor wire around its roof.

From the doorway upstairs, I'm facing two storeys of cells overlooking a day room with shower cubicles at the end of both tiers. At two white plastic circular tables, prisoners are playing dominoes, cards, chess and Scrabble, some concentrating, others yelling obscenities, contributing to a brain-scraping din that I hope to block out by purchasing a Walkman. In a raised box-shaped Plexiglas control tower, two guards are monitoring the prisoners.

Bud returns. My pulse jumps. Not wanting to feel like I'm stuck in a kennel with a rabid dog, I grab a notepad and pen and head for the day room.

Focussed on my body language, not wanting to signal any weakness, I'm striding along the upper tier, head and chest elevated, when two hands appear from a doorway and grab me. I drop the pad. The pen clinks against grid-metal and tumbles to the day room as I'm pulled into a cell reeking of backside sweat and masturbation, a cheese-tinted funk.

"I'm Booga. Let's fuck," says a squat man in urine-stained boxers, with WHITE TRASH tattooed on his torso below a mobile home, and an arm sleeved with the Virgin Mary.

Shocked, I brace to flee or fight to preserve my anal virginity. I can't believe my eyes when he drops his boxers and waggles his penis.

Dancing to music playing through a speaker he has rigged up, Booga smiles in a sexy way. "Come on," he says in a husky voice. "Drop your pants. Let's fuck." He pulls pornography faces. I question his sanity. He moves closer. "If I let you fart in my mouth, can I fart in yours?"

"You can fuck off," I say, springing towards the doorway.

He grabs me. We scuffle. Every time I make progress towards the doorway, he clings to my clothes, dragging me back in. When I feel his penis rub against my leg, my adrenalin kicks in so forcefully I experience a burst of strength and wriggle free. I bolt out as fast as my shower sandals will allow and snatch my pad. Looking over my shoulder, I see him stood calmly in the doorway, smiling. He points at me. "You have to walk past my door every day. We're gonna get together. I'll lick your ass and you can fart in my mouth." Booga blows a kiss and disappears.

I rush downstairs. With my back to a wall, I pause to steady my thoughts and breathing. In survival mode, I think, *What's going to come at me next?* In the hope of reducing my tension, I borrow a pen to do what helps me stay sane: writing. With the details fresh in my mind, I document my journey to the prison for my blog readers, keeping an eye out in case anyone else wants to test the new prisoner. The more I write, the more I fill with a sense of purpose. Jon's Jail Journal is a connection to the outside world that I cherish.

Someone yells, "One time!" The din lowers. A door rumbles

open. A guard does a security walk, his every move scrutinised by dozens of scornful eyes staring from cells. When he exits, the din resumes, and the prisoners return to injecting drugs to escape from reality, including the length of their sentences. This continues all day with "Two times!" signifying two approaching guards, and "Three times!" three and so on. Every now and then an announcement by a guard over the speakers briefly lowers the din.

Before lockdown, I join the line for a shower, holding bars of soap in a towel that I aim to swing at the head of the next person to try me. With boisterous inmates a few feet away, yelling at the men in the showers to "Stop jerking off," and "Hurry the fuck up," I get in a cubicle that reeks of bleach and mildew. With every nerve strained, I undress and rinse fast.

At night, despite the desert heat, I cocoon myself in a blanket from head to toe and turn towards the wall, making my face more difficult to strike. I leave a hole for air, but the warm cement block inches from my mouth returns each exhalation to my face as if it's breathing on me, creating a feeling of suffocation. For hours, my heart drums so hard against the thin mattress I feel as if I'm moving even though I'm still. I try to sleep, but my eyes keep springing open and my head turning towards the cell as I try to penetrate the darkness, searching for Bud swinging a padlock in a sock at my head.

Printed in Great Britain
by Amazon